UNLEASHING THE
POWER OF PEOPLE

A Guide to Organizing People and Systems

JEFFREY HOWE, PhD

outskirtspress

DENVER, COLORADO

Special Thanks to Patrick O'Brien and Eric Bloomquist, great friends and mentors - without whom this book never could have occurred.

Acknowledgments

I want to thank my reviewers, especially Jim Bowyer, Steve Bratkovich, Patrick O'Brien, Steve Rohde, Collin Miller, Tim Downing, Katie Fernholz, and Matt Frank, for their support and input on this project.

I also want to thank a number of people that were critical to the experiential learning part of this book, including Alison Garside, Ann (Connor) Bloomquist, Don Heise, Phil Steklenski, Lucy Voltz, Mike Bryant, and Tim Pepera.

Table of Contents

Preface

This book evolved out of forty plus years of experience with, and research[1] on thousands of companies. Much of this was focused on the forest products sector, although during the last 15 years this broadened to organizations of all kind, from architecture to restaurants, recreation, and education. Through good times, boom times, recessions and a great recession, the lessons remain the same; happy people lead to happy companies and the result is a level of success beyond expectation. When people like working for a company they tend to be more flexible, more accepting of change, and work harder to improve themselves and the organization. If they trust that the company really cares, they link their happiness to that of the organization. It's been said that, *"caring, in a world gone numb is an almost unfair advantage."*[2] Nowhere is this more evident than in the workplace.

I have been very fortunate to be part of some amazing successes. I've seen a struggling cooking school blossom into a creative regional power influencing national health insurance companies and nutrition in the workplace…and becoming extremely profitable in the process. I've also seen a small furniture company turn *within a year* from the most hated place to work in their community to an employer of choice, by focusing on their people skills, and leading to record profitability. And I've seen a manufacturing company reduce lead times from months to hours, inventory from millions to a few hundred thousand, late deliveries from many to zero, while increasing quality performance, decreasing price to the customer, increasing sku's and quadrupling profits; all by focusing on interpersonal communication. The company workplace was such a caring, creative culture that the Ernst-Young Entrepreneur of the Year award committee noted that they had never seen such happy, enthusiastic group of people. It's easier to envision the possibilities when you've seen them occur.

In many ways happiness is a major goal of highly successful organizations… recognizing that the things that make us happy - a sense of belonging to a community, opportunities to create, learn and grow, and a feeling that you are in the "flow" of life – are the same characteristics that make great employees. Gandhi said, *"Happiness is when what you think, what you say, and what you do are in harmony."*[3] Basically this defines the purpose of this book… to ensure that you have the processes, methods, and tools to bring harmony and prosperity to your organization.

Jeff Howe

Introduction
Read me first!

The purpose of this book is to provide a step-by-step guide to developing your leadership skills and those of other key individuals in your organization in order to significantly increase sales, profits, and personal satisfaction. What kinds of organization does this approach apply to? It is particularly aimed at:

- Privately owned (E.g. owner-operators)
- Family owned
- Private Investor owned
- ESOPS

And it applies to all categories within a given sector including consulting firms, primary and secondary manufacturers, wholesale, retail, and installers. Most of the information in this book is also applicable to nonprofits and government organizations, although the examples focus on experiences of for-profit companies.

This book is based on more than 40 years of leadership experience as well as years of research into what separates highly successful companies from the herd. The goal of this book is to help you make a big difference in your organization (or your part) *immediately*. This book is not about theory, although theory is discussed; it is about immediately implementing the kinds of activities that will make the biggest difference in your organization.

The reality is you can completely change your organization in less than a year... *if you make it a priority*. By change I am referring to things like: fostering happy,

If you don't have a plan for where you want to go and how to get there, you have to live with where you end up!

motivated, accountable people, reduced lead times, higher quality, and greater profitability. Follow the guidelines in this book fully and the change will be dramatic.

However, success isn't inevitable. Generally, leaders that are struggling to achieve the kind of success they desire are experiencing a failure of some kind. These failures can broadly be described as:

<u>Failure to gather input</u> – believing you have to solve all your own problems can not only lead to insufficient solutions, but also isolation, loneliness, frustration, and anger at others. To solve things quickly you need to admit you need help, seek it from those around you or from other experts, and then truly listen to what they say. Generally to get a different result than what is currently going on, you have to do something different. What that is, you might not be able to imagine, but others might. The earlier you ask for help in the planning process the better your plan and the more likely you are not only to achieve it but to get motivated help in implementing it.

<u>Failure to commit</u> – by not clearly declaring your goals you demonstrate a lack of commitment to achieving them. Sure the world is a fluid place, but inaction never got you anywhere. Research has shown that the old saying, "think, speak, and do" has great validity in achieving success. Those individuals and organizations that clearly declare what they want are far more likely to get it. Organizational vision and individual purpose are examples of clear commitments.

<u>Failure to Plan</u> - individuals and organizations fail to write down plans for a lot of reasons, the big one often being that there hasn't been commitment to anything, thus making change difficult if not impossible to plan for. But if you commit to what you want to achieve, clearly the next step is

to plan how to get there. And like commitments, plans are much more successful when you write them down and share with everyone involved. Basically what you are saying is, "I want this and here is how I am going to get it."

Failure to monitor, evaluate, and adjust – The key to a successful plan is in recognizing it is a living, breathing guide not a prescription. Thus progress must be monitored, evaluated against plan, and activities adjusted as necessary. Just because everything isn't going the way you thought doesn't mean you give up on your goals. It just means you now know more than you did and you adjust activities to get back on track. Generally this is done at least quarterly with some adjustments done monthly. Proactive leaders are constantly adjusting to changing situations, but their overall goals don't change, just how they get there.

> So, basically the keys to success, and the objectives of this book, are:
> ✓ Have a plan (written)
> ✓ Implement plan (monitor and adjust regularly)
> ✓ Do it collectively not singularly (facilitate people)
> ✓ Consistently improve (both people and systems)
> ✓ Communicate, communicate, communicate

Deciding what you want to achieve in life, planning on how to achieve it, getting others to help you achieve your goals, and then monitoring and adjusting activities to make it happen are the fundamental principles of both life and business that we too often take for granted. Interestingly, personal happiness and organizational success are linked; and when you can link personal goals, and passion, with organizational goals great things can happen. You can truly change your world!

Framework of the book

This book provides a people-centric approach to organizational success. The fundamental purpose of this book is to enhance your leadership skills and guide you in achieving your goals. Good communication skills are critical to great leadership, and *the annual plan is the foundation for all organizational communication.* Therefore, some of the basic outcomes of this book are a written annual plan and the process and tools needed to guide implementation and achievement of that plan. Both the process and the experience in developing and implementing this plan will significantly enhance your leadership skills over a very short period of time. Leaders report that they have seen dramatic changes in themselves and their organization's performance in a year or less after development of and commitment to a written plan.

Leaders depend on excellent interpersonal communication skills. So to assure you can accomplish the tasks outlined in the balance of the book, the first two chapters of the book provide you with two core skills that will increase your likelihood of success.

In any organization time is money, and time management is an important skill. **Chapter 1** introduces you to some *facilitation* skills that ensure your time spent with others is efficient, effective, and fosters collaboration. **Chapter 2** introduces a *communication_process*, the Mobius Model,[4] which gives you a new positive, constructive way to look at communication between two or more individuals and to manage that process to ensure positive outcomes. The tools described in the first two chapters can be and *should be applied immediately* and you will see an immediate impact! The Mobius is also utilized in a number of other chapters to demonstrate its use and to enhance learning.

There are often a variety of perspectives about what is going on in an organization. The ability to assess and come to an agreement on what is truly important to do in an organization is critically important to achieving real and dramatic improvement. **Chapter 3** discusses a fairly quick and straightforward way to apply skills learned in Chapters 1 & 2 in an assessment process that consolidates wide input to achieve agreement and collaboration toward organizational improvement.

Two models are also introduced: *The Fifth Discipline*[5] and the *Organizational Systems Model* to help visualize the important parts and pieces of your organization that need assessment and aid in clearly defining, prioritizing, and communicating areas for improvement. The Assessment process will have immediate impact on individuals within the organization. The important part is truly listening and responding. By publicly tracking recommendations and ticking them off as you address them you build support and commitment to improvement. Never underestimate the power of the little things!

Chapter 4 introduces Planning as an important system in an organization, and the development of strategic, marketing, operational, financial, organizational and annual business plans. The development, communication, monitoring and celebration of the achievement of plan goals are a central part of organizing your company to succeed.

Chapter 5 is primarily aimed at the top leader of the organization. If you are a top leader and are trying to make significant change and improve the likelihood of success of your organization you probably need help. Research [6] indicates that the sharing of leadership is a crucial component of successfully making a significant change in the fortunes of the organization. Chapter 5 discusses the formation of a leadership team in order to establish and implement a comprehensive plan quickly and effectively.

The foundation of all organizational communication rests on the plan.   If you don't know what you are trying to accomplish how can you expect people to help you? **Chapter 6 and 7** take the results from the assessment and lead you step-by-step through a speedy process to develop both strategic and action plans for the year (together often called the business plan or annual plan).

Chapters 8 and 9 are designed to introduce and clarify the role of marketing in the organization. Chapter 8, Marketing 101, introduces you to all the basics of how marketing can strategically guide your organization to higher levels of success. Chapter 9 delves into the step-by-step specifics of growing sales of the right product to the right people.

Chapters 10, 11, and 12 describe the fundamental components of your operational, financial, and human resource systems. A number of tools and unique approaches are included in these chapters that show how to address specific situations and to ensure that clear communication, clear expectations and clear agreements exist to meet the needs of all stakeholders.

Finally, **Chapter 13** briefly discusses the implementation, monitoring and adjustment process that guides achievement of the annual plan. Plans are simply guides to what you want to achieve. A mediocre plan well implemented is much better than a great plan poorly implemented. Thus a process is suggested to ensure people persist in seeking desired end results and adjust activities as necessary to changing conditions in order to stay on track.

This book is designed in a way that allows each segment to be used independently. You do not have to read this book from start to finish in order to find value. It is recommended, but not necessary. So if, for example, you are simply looking for way to tune up your sales, or simply need a wage and incentive system, you can jump directly to the marketing or human resources segments of the book and get some detailed guidance.

Yet a business shouldn't be a cluster of discrete ideas, tools and resources. The real value in this book is in how all the pieces work together, and the recognition that all the equipment, the inventory, the assets, and most importantly, the people can be interwoven together in a way that makes the whole more valuable than the sum of its parts. The net result is in a higher state of well-being for the three primary stakeholders in any organization, the owners - the employees, and the business itself; and this higher well-being benefits the surrounding community as well. Happiness spreads like wildfire.

Now read on!

Chapter 1
Critical Leadership Skills: Communication, Facilitation, Collaboration, and Conflict Resolution

Businesses are about people. It is not the equipment that makes you money, it is the decision to buy it, the decision of when to turn it on or off, what to feed it, how hard to push it, and when to let it rest; these and other major decisions are all directly or indirectly made by people. If you know your priorities you will make better decisions, and the more successful the business. It's that simple really. Really!

The old adage "great leaders are born, not made" is just not true. Great leadership is the sum of our experiences, skills, education, training, and development. Great leaders identify clear role models, successful practices, effective systems, and personal behaviors that result in success in the organization. Like it or not, as leaders you are role models for the rest of the staff. As you do, so shall they. And if you're the top leader, owner or CEO - your behaviors have the greatest influence – both for good or bad.

> *"The employees in the manufacturing plant work just as hard 40 hours a week whether we in the office make good decisions or bad. To make their efforts valuable we need to make good ones."*
> ...Eric Bloomquist, Owner
> Colonial Craft

To become a great role model it is critical that leaders become confidently self-aware. Self-aware means you understand your personal strength and weaknesses. "Confidently self-aware" indicates that you are mindful, vulnerable, face your weaknesses and address them. Most

1

leaders today are familiar with a SWOT analysis (strengths, weaknesses, opportunities, and threats). But they rarely apply this to themselves. Good decisions are more likely when individuals are able to honestly evaluate themselves and the climate they compete in. A good leader must be constantly self-evaluating his or herself toward continuous improvement.

Great leaders are not perfect. A great strength is in their recognition of their weaknesses and having the confidence to build a team around them that complement, and supplement, their abilities. I would note that neither Bill Gates nor Steve Jobs started their famous enterprises, Apple and Microsoft respectively, alone. They knew they needed other and different skills. A great idea, poorly implemented is… well just an idea. A great idea, well implemented can change the world. Investing time, energy, and resources in developing leadership skills will change your world.

What skills are needed? Do you need to go back to school and finish that MBA? Not necessarily. To compete in today's fast-paced world an organization's highest priority is to share leadership. The primary skills that need to be developed by leaders to make that happen are dominantly interpersonal. These include: invitation, communication, facilitation, collaboration, and conflict resolution. In this book I shall use the following definitions:

<u>Invitation</u> – is the process of engaging people in achieving goals and objectives through motivation and creating a shared interest in outcomes. Good invitations pull people forward rather than push or force the issue. Daniel Pink points out in his book "Drive" that employees need to feel

To organize and collaborate you must learn to facilitate and communicate!

connected to a larger company goal or purpose.[7] The

company vision, mission and values are the foundational invitation a leader makes. *Chapter 6 provides a detailed discussion on creating an organizational vision, mission, and values statements.*

Communication – is the process of transferring information between all affected parties such that organizational objectives are achieved effectively and efficiently. The goal of good communication is that every individual is making the best decisions possible based on the most complete information available. *The balance of this chapter introduces the Mobius communication model, as a process for guiding constructive and successful communication.*

Facilitation – is the process of coordinating individuals (or groups of individuals) to optimize the achievement of the group's (or organization's) objectives. The goal of facilitation is the highest level of collaboration possible. *In Chapter 2 I will explore some tools that will help develop your facilitation skills.*

Collaboration – is the process of individuals (or groups) working in concert such that the whole is greater than the sum of its parts. That is, you are able to achieve a higher level of success by working together and coordinating than if you were all operating independently. *Collaboration is the outcome of good communication and facilitation.*

Conflict resolution – is the process of resolving and integrating multiple perspectives (critical to collaboration) such that the result is comprehensive rather than iterative. It is not necessarily about disagreement, but rather about bringing various points of view (e.g. representatives of different functions such as sales and operations) to solutions consider and implement based on all aspects of the situation. *Conflict resolution is addressed in Chapter 12 on Human Resources.*

3

Leaders also need to be persistent in seeking to achieve outcomes, develop both their own creative natures and support the creativity of the organization, and not be afraid to make mistakes. These three characteristics (persistence, creativity, and fearlessness) are inexorably linked. Great leaders don't give up on a goal just because one approach didn't work. They welcome new ideas and aren't afraid to try new things.

Communication as a Process: The Mobius Model

Good communication doesn't happen accidentally and without practice. However, it is a skill that can fairly easily be developed. To foster good communication it is helpful to have a guide or path that maximizes the potential for good communication to occur. On the following page is an image adapted from the Mobius Model, a communication tool originally developed by William Stockton, PhD, based on his research into what made groups of people get the most done, the quickest and most successfully.[4] He found that there was a clear sequence of events that: fully engaged people in a process, collaboratively incorporated multiple perspectives and ideas simultaneously, and motivated individuals to accomplish group goals and objectives.

Stockton found that one of the benefits of the sequence was that it provided both the process and the safety for individuals to voice both their creative intuitive (and often internal) ideas and their rational external thoughts to address the issue at hand. He named his model after the individual that discovered the Mobius strip or infinity loop, which is an object that appears to have two sides but actually only has one (see image below).[8] The goal is that individuals engaged in the process bring out their inner thoughts, concerns, and ideas such that they are part of the single, overall discussion.

4

As adapted herein, the Mobius Model can be used as a tool in specific situations (e.g. planning or conflict resolution) or as simply a way of thinking. Organizations that adopt the Mobius Model find that it dramatically modifies behavior. People quickly recognize the efficacy of getting input from others on both the situation and possible solutions, as

© Oninegranhics

well as getting agreement from those involved before proceeding to action. It is simply way more effective and, as the old adage suggests, "success breeds success." The Mobius is a subtle tool with huge implications. It is a tool that not only can be used for better communication, but also results in naturally collaborative processes. It can also used as a process to resolve both minor and serious conflicts. Thus, the basic concepts and framework are introduced in this chapter, and then expanded upon in greater detail and demonstrated through examples in subsequent chapters.

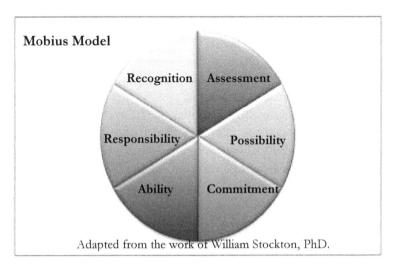

Mobius Model

Recognition · Assessment · Responsibility · Possibility · Ability · Commitment

Adapted from the work of William Stockton, PhD.

As shown in the figure above, the Mobius Model has six steps. In this discussion they are referred to as:

1. Coming to a Mutual Understanding of the Situation (Mutual Understanding or "<u>Assessment</u>")
2. Defining Possibilities (<u>Possibilities</u>)
3. Clarifying Commitment to the Best Options (<u>Commitment</u>)
4. Agreeing to an Action Plan (Action Plans or "<u>Ability</u>")
5. Agreeing on Individual Responsibilities (<u>Responsibility</u>)
6. Evaluating Progress & Celebrating Accomplishment (<u>Recognition</u>)

As with the Mobius loop itself the model is meant to be continuous; that is once you have completed a sequence you assess and move on to the next highest priority. You can also apply the model so specific issues without need for a broad assessment of the whole.

1. <u>Assessment</u>: the first step in the Mobius communication model is to come to a mutual understanding of what is going on. Ideally you gather the broadest number of individual  perspectives possible, in confidence, from those involved. This is often called the *assessment* phase, and in many ways is similar to a traditional organizational assessment, except that it can be applied to virtually any situation where two or more people are in communication. The major difference is in the language. The goal of the mutual understanding phase is to define a higher level of *well-being* for the issue at hand. So, in the case of organizational planning (for example), you might be trying to define what could be done within a given time

period to make the organization a happier, more profitable place.

Two questions are used to foster positive results and clear communication. Examples of these are:

1. *What is present that contributes to the well-being of the organization?*
2. *What is missing that if it were present would lead to a higher level of well-being over the next year?*

By gathering summarized lists of what is present and missing from stakeholders (potentially including important vendors and customers) you get a broad view of what is going well and individuals value, and what you can do to make the situation better. For greater value, the missing elements can be prioritized to guide what to work on in the timeframe at hand.

2. Defining <u>Possibilities</u>: Next the organization must take the organized, prioritized missing elements, turn them into possibilities, and decide which ones can be collectively addressed over the next year. To do that effectively it is important to clarify what people's individual view of success looks like.

To define success in addressing a specific "missing" the question that is asked is, "how would we know we succeeded?" William Stockton described these responses as "Conditions of Satisfaction." That is, individuals would be

To turn a "missing" into a "possibility" you simply state it in the positive. Thus, if "a clear vision statement" is missing, then "a clear and written vision statement exists" would be the possibility.

7

happy with the outcome under certain, often unspecified, conditions. It is here that you want to specify them openly and in detail (because these will lead to action items) and as long as there isn't a direct conflict between them (e.g. one person wants blue and another wants red as a condition) everyone does not have to believe a condition is important to include it. It just has to be important to one person.

Conditions of Satisfaction (COS) should be defined for each highly ranked possibility. In some cases there may only be one condition for a possibility - not all missing things people think are important are complicated. In other cases there may be as many as ten conditions attached to an individual possibility. Once you have defined these COS (or success factors) for each important possibility you can decide which possibility(s) the organization can commit to addressing in the next year.

3. Clarifying Commitment: The third step in the process is to determine which of the possibilities the organization is willing and able to commit to. Note that at this point you have  not decided exactly what you are going to do or who's going to do it, only that the item is very important, and you have clarified what each person's view of success looks like. Thus this is a strategic issue rather than functional one at this point. So the question you are answering here is, *"which of these possibilities are important enough, and would make the greatest difference, if addressed in the next year?"*

Commitment should NOT be a passive act.[10] The first two steps on the Mobius are very collaborative and this one needs to be as well. Ideally you are looking for those possibilities that the entire group can support as being important. Although there are situations where the <u>top leader</u>

may add to the final list (meaning endorsing and retaining a possibility others don't feel is as important), she or he should refrain from reducing the list (that is, overruling what the rest of the group thinks is important). Commitment to a given possibility should be by a verbal or physical (e.g. show of hands) vote. There should be no neutral parties – you are either for or against, and no non-response acceptance – everyone must physically respond somehow. People that are reluctant to commit

Five Finger Voting:
Have each person vote by raising a number of fingers of one hand based on their interest as follows:
✓ *5 fingers - Love it*
✓ *4 fingers - It's very good*
✓ *3 fingers - It's fine*
✓ *2 fingers - I need more info to support it*
✓ *1 finger - I can't support it*

physically often have a condition of satisfaction that is missing from the list for a given possibility. Requiring people to physically act helps to stimulate a clarifying discussion about that condition of satisfaction.[11]

Once you have determined which of the possibilities are strategically important for the organization to address in the next year you have a strategic plan. The possibilities you have committed to are now

The strategic planning process does not need to take a lot of time. In 2-3 days you can have a plan that can change the future of the organization!

the core *strategies* you are going to put your time and effort into in the coming year, and the COSs are organizational *objectives*. This information should be shared with *at least* everyone involved in the assessment phase and preferably the entire organization. Next you need to define the actions necessary to implement these strategies and achieve those objectives. This takes the form of a traditional action plan.

Good strategies should foster a dialogue about the many ideas and opinions on how to get things done.

4. Ability: Agreeing to actions – Most leaders are very familiar with an action plan. The action plan is at the heart of the traditional individual problem-solving approach to planning in many organizations.  This approach often involves identification of a single individual who is informed in one way or another "it's your job to figure it out and fix it." This approach, which skips Mobius steps 2 and 3, or sometimes 1-3, means the result is totally dependent on the skills, ingenuity, and knowledge of that one person. While this approach may occasionally be effective, more often than not the result is inadequate or incomplete problem solving and, worse, reluctance on the part of employees to identify problems at all. The "figure it out and fix it" approach often means that big problems just get reduced and small problems accumulate to often bubble up again later.

If you compare this approach to that with the more successful communication model, what you see is that we have basically been taught to skip the gathering of other people's perspectives, the development of a comprehensive view of success, and any formal commitment to the best solution. In fact, in the last twenty years American leaders have been taught to completely skip the whole right side of the Mobius. Who hasn't heard the saying, "don't bring me problems, bring me solutions?" This approach forces people to work in isolation, creates a process that is highly iterative (suggesting that as long as you're making progress on solving the problem you are being successful), and virtually eliminates an organization's opportunity, and perhaps ability to change and adapt to situations such as increased foreign competition.

Clearly it is far better to take a few more minutes up front and solve the problem once and for all.

In the Mobius Model the action plan simply describes what needs to happen by when in order to implement the strategies defined in the first three steps and meet the COS defined in step two. Action items are fairly obvious if the COS are clear.

It is important to note that at this point you still haven't decided who is going to do what!! Why is that so? Because one goal of this sequence is to recognize three important things: First, you don't want to limit the development of ideas to only those who have time or specific skill by routinely assigning responsibility to those who had the idea - thereby teaching bright, busy people and bright people that don't have specific skills or training related to an issue, to not have ideas. Second, you don't want to assign responsibility until you know the skills needed (e.g. actions required) and timelines. Third, you don't want to limit yourself to current resources sitting at the table. IF an issue or need is important enough for the organization to commit to it then you will want to think outside the box on how to get it done, e.g. hire a temporary person, a consultant, or use someone from a different part of the organization. You want to be as creative as possible.

5. Agreeing on <u>Responsibility</u>: The responsibility step is a combination of assigning and accepting responsibility (or becoming "champion") for certain strategies or  actions. To accomplish this effectively you must consider skills, experience, and available time. In this step it is not uncommon to swap other responsibilities in order to take on a new one. That is, in order for a person to champion the

new critical strategy with the given timelines they need to hand off some other responsibility or group of tasks and/or the timeline may need to be adjusted. The first time this process is done in a organization we find that a lot of "tasks" get passed to direct reports as leaders begin working on activities with broader implications for the organization. In some cases leaders begin working on the "right" things for the first time! Often, we also find people consciously or subconsciously accept a sort of "conditional" responsibility. That is, they accept responsibility for an action, with voiced or unvoiced reservations dependent on its complexity as they get into it. Sort of "we'll worry about that when we get to it" approach. The benchmarking decisions made in step six help address this.

It is not unusual to get to this point in the process and find that no one wants to accept responsibility for an action. Usually this means you have missed some conditions of satisfaction for the strategy, and you have to back up just on that specific item and add some conditions of satisfaction that address why people won't volunteer (addressing the issue, "*I can't volunteer unless this (COS) and that (COS) occur.*") These are critical clarification steps and another of the reasons you wait until all the actions are described before defining responsibility.

6. <u>Recognition</u>: – this step is all about benchmarking progress and celebrating when stages or actions are complete. It is also the stage in the process when you define "how  will we know progress is occurring?" This step clarifies responsibilities in general since the identification of intermediate benchmarks (i.e. to complete this action we would need to be at this point by this date) more clearly defines potential time conflicts for the person responsible.

As noted above, it is at this point champions negotiate the timing, priority, and responsibility for tasks that they have and the need for additional human resources is often evaluated.

Another big question is how will the planning group know that benchmarks have been achieved? This question is both about information sharing and accountability. It is reasonable for items of low importance to be communicated simply by posting a notice or sending emails. However, items of high importance should be evaluated and celebrated face to face. People are much more likely to complete projects if they must report into a group on their progress.

Most businesses have enough action items to complete, and enough intermediate benchmarks that a monthly meeting of the planning group is valuable to measure progress, celebrate completion of projects, and adjust activities as necessary. The last thing you want to occur is for an important project to get derailed by changing priorities of an individual when the original project is still a high priority of the organization. It is much easier to meet at a regularly planned time and at regular intervals than to randomly organize meetings as needed. You can always cancel unnecessary meetings, but spending time trying to fit an unscheduled meeting into a group of 4-12 people's busy schedules can be a big waste of time for everyone. The process of agreeing to keep the morning of the third Wednesday of every month available takes five minutes, once.

Backwards Conversations
It's important to recognize there are many negative conversations that occur between individuals, and these can be a source of creativity if addressed. These "blame" or "fault-based" conversations leave both parties equally unhappy and the issues unresolved or magnified. These blame conversations are generally based on historical experience between the parties and tend to focus on: what's

wrong (Recognition), who's at fault (Responsibility), and what they should do to fix it (Ability). The result is that you have a backwards communication process that results in: compliance rather than Commitment, scorekeeping rather than a Possibility of true resolution (and people accumulate a parking lot of issues between each other), and divisiveness and a we/they attitude instead of organizational Well-being.

The creative opportunity, in backwards conversations, is to translate those things that are "wrong" into what's missing and, ultimately, possibilities. This leads not only to the possibility of resolving the issue at hand but also beginning to address the history behind the relationship; ultimately leading to a higher state of well-being for the parties involved and those around them.

Summary

The Mobius Model fosters clear communication and collaboration. The clear communication comes as a result of formatted stages that result in clear expectations and clear agreements leading to clear outcomes that are monitored and celebrated. The Model fosters collaboration by gathering input from a wide range of perspectives, integrating that input into final solutions and actions, gaining commitment from individuals on priorities of the group, while measuring progress and celebrating success.

In succeeding chapters the use of the Mobius in developing plans and motivating employees toward achieving organizational objectives will be explained. The value of the Mobius in a performance review will also be demonstrated as will its use as a conflict resolution tool (Chapter 12) to help address disagreement between two or more individuals in an organization.

14

Chapter 2
Art & Science of Facilitation

Many people report that they spend more than half their time in meetings and that a vast majority of that time is wasted. We know that time spent in groups is both the most expensive time we spend and potentially the most valuable if collaborative. It is important to make that time effective. *Facilitation is the process of "making things easier" and "coordinating the work of a group of people,"* ideally both. There are some fundamental meeting management skills that any leader can learn quickly and will improve meetings dramatically. For this book a meeting is defined as: any time two or more people are in direct concurrent[12] communication.

As with all communication management processes the primary outcomes are: clear expectations and clear agreements leading to clear outcomes. The following meeting management methods may seem simple but can completely alter the effectiveness of an organization. In my work, it is common to hear from organizations that have implemented this approach that, "we can't imagine a time when we didn't use these methods... they make such a difference." These basic methods or tools are shown in the box below.

The discussion in the balance of this chapter is designed to help you adopt these skills immediately!! I recommend you begin implementing these tools as soon as possible, ideally within 48 hours of reading this! These tools ensure an efficient and effective planning process, and business.

15

- *Clear and agreed upon ground rules for operating in groups*
- *Clear and agreed on agendas for any meeting, with:*
    - *Clear champion for each item (who's going to lead discussion?)*
    - *Clear outcomes for each item (what do we want to achieve with this discussion?)*
    - *Clear time expectations for each item (how long do we expect this to take?)*
    - *Clear process for discussion (e.g. brainstorm, vote, open discussion, structured discussion)*
- *Agreed on facilitator and scribe role for any meeting*
- *Agreed on tools such as the "Action-Decision Register"*

Ground Rules

It is critical that every organization have clear and agreed on ground rules for meetings. Individual teams that meet regularly can adopt those ground rules and expand on them as needed or, if organizational versions are nonexistent, teams should adopt their own. All ground rules should be based on the core values of the organization (e.g. a respect for people's time) and are focused on making the time spent together meaningful. Example ground rules commonly adopted include:

We agree to…
- Meet and end on time
- Use facilitation/meeting management tools
- Provide the agenda at least 24 hours in advance so people can prepare
- Use a facilitator and a scribe, and that those roles are shared and rotate throughout the year[13]

- One person speaks at a time
- Everything discussed is confidential without the expressed agreement of individual involved
- Ensure each individual is able to take care of themselves (physically, mentally, emotionally and spiritually)
- The "group" or team has a clear purpose or role within the organization (What is the primary reason for this team to meet regularly?)
- Individuals support the decisions of the group with others in the organization (e.g. you may disagree behind closed doors but must create a united front to the balance of organization once decisions are made.)

Each individual should clearly acknowledge and agree to support the ground rules of the group at the formative meeting of that group or at the time of their addition to the group. Accountability to best practices occurs when agreement is clear and shared. Many organizations post their ground rules in regular meeting spaces for reinforcement.

Agenda

The purpose of the agenda is to 1) focus the discussions of the group on areas of greatest importance and those that are pertinent to the collective members, and 2) for the sharing of information when you want all parties to be sure to hear the same information the same way at the same time to avoid any confusion. Topics can be as wide ranging as measuring performance toward financial goals, to obtaining collective advice on how to handle a complex employee situation.

To facilitate meetings it is valuable to have standing agenda items that are specifically designed to lead to more efficient meeting experiences. These include at beginning of meeting:

- Check-in [14] (each person briefly answers two questions: How are they and is there anything in the way of their being fully present?)
- Review of previous action items from previous meeting

At the end of meeting:

- Review of actions and decisions recorded from current meeting
- Checkout (Each person briefly answers two questions: What was present that made the meeting go well and what was missing that would have made it a better meeting?)

The purpose of the *check-in* is to help guide the facilitator in understanding both the behavior of the participants and the needed sequence of agenda items. As an example, it is helpful for the facilitator and the group to know if an individual doesn't feel well or had something dramatic, either positive or negative happen that is affecting them. Having someone sitting there looking mad when they are actually sick can be a big and unnecessary distraction to the group. Also, things always pop up for busy people, so if someone has a crisis they need to address they can report it up front and the facilitator can adjust the agenda sequence to help that person and the group make best use of each other's time and the affected person leave early if needed.

By reviewing *previous action items* from the past meeting at the beginning of each meeting you hold people accountable to what they agreed to do. Experience shows that when people know they are going to be asked if they did what they promised at the beginning of the meeting they almost always complete the task.

Reviewing *current action items* at the end of a meeting as well as decisions made during the meeting clarifies what people have agreed to do and by when, and clearly defines exactly what decisions were made. This reinforces *clear agreements* by the group and *clear expectations* of each individual.

The *checkout process* ensures the continuous improvement of group meetings. It is this process that points out all the little details that make things get really efficient over time. Check out comments like – "I wish we had received the data in advance to review," or "the pictures and graphs were really helpful in understanding what was going on," or especially, "I think we got off track too many times and could have been more efficient with our time" can lead to both direct and subtle improvements that make expensive time spent together more effective and efficient... and potentially fun.

In general, the four standard items described above shouldn't take a total of more than 10-15 minutes out of a 2-hour meeting, depending on the size of the group. Naturally, you have to tailor this process to the size of the group and the length of the meeting.

The balance of the meeting should be spent dominantly engaged in the following processes:

- Gathering Input
- Brainstorming and/or developing ideas
- Coordinating activities
- Sharing information
- Making decisions on issues that affect the entire group
- Setting collective goals and objectives
- Holding each other accountable (reviewing activities and adjusting as needed to meet goals)
- Dialogue, or exchange of opinions and ideas

19

Facilitator & Scribe

The primary role of the facilitator is to gather and disseminate the agenda according to the ground rules, guide the group in sequencing the agenda topics, manage the discussion process for a topic to ensure people are engaged and that a desired outcome is achieved, manage the meeting time by tracking the time spent on individual agenda items, and lead the check-in and checkout processes. In high-performing teams the facilitator will hand off facilitation of a particular agenda item if they are personally engaged in that topic to ensure times are still managed and the process is still effective.

An experienced facilitator will also coach team members on the development and clarification of proposed end-results and a best process to achieve those results. They will also provide input on interpersonal issues that come up during meetings such as willingness to take a risk (e.g. to voice a concern) and on how to address control dramas. Control dramas are tactics of manipulation that everyone has learned early in life as a means of getting his or her way, and can be addressed through redirecting of the individual toward a more constructive method.

The scribe's job is to maintain the Action-Decision Register to ensure collective agreement on group decisions and individual commitments. Each individual may take notes on items of personal interest, but the scribe tracks any decision and any task that any individual agrees to take on. It is best if the scribe role is rotated between people from meeting to meeting as it is a great training activity for the communication skill of clarifying and writing down what an individual agrees to do. The scribe is the champion on the standing action-decision register items on the agenda. At the beginning of the meeting they review all agreed on actions from the previous meeting to ensure completion and they review the actions and agreements captured from the current meeting.

20

Action-Decision Register

The action-decision register is a deceptively simple tool that when combined with the review process is *probably the most important activity that an organization can adopt immediately*! A sample is included in the Appendix, but the action-decision register is simply a formatted document that is filled in every meeting. On the action portion are places for champion, action, due date, and defer date. Groups do not champion actions. If a group is going to take on an action, then one person should be assigned to facilitate that group (e.g. schedule meetings) and that person would be the champion. This creates a clear responsibility for the action.

Action items and completion date are pretty self-explanatory. The defer date may be a less familiar term for readers. The defer date on an action-decision register acknowledges that there may be some instances where a task is incomplete for good reason. Thus at the succeeding meeting a new or "deferred" date is set for completing the activity. However, a subtle part of the action-decision register is that there is only a spot for one deferral date. As a guideline, if a person cannot complete a task by the second completion date, this becomes a new agenda item and the task is reviewed for importance and if still important to the group, a new champion is considered. In practice this rarely happens more than once. People become more realistic about due dates, better discussions occur about exactly what is needed and important, and people rarely miss a due date once much less twice. Peer pressure is a great tool for ensuring personal responsibility and accountability.

> *"I can't believe we survived without this tool! It use to be people were always delaying activities, or partially completing them, or not doing some of them at all, or even doing something completely different than we thought we agreed on.*

At the end of the meeting the written actions are reviewed and the champion is responding to three things:

- Is the action captured accurately and clearly?
- Is the date the agreed on date?
- Is the champion committed to completing it by that date?

This is the opportunity to clarify language, such as "I didn't say I would complete the project by tomorrow. I said I'd get the team formed to start work on it by tomorrow. The project will actually be complete in two weeks." This may foster further discussion or simply be tweaking of the terminology and dates.

The decision portion of the register simply captures those decisions made by the group that affect the whole. Group decisions are not meant to replace the responsibility of an individual to do their job and make decisions in their individual role. They are meant to document decisions that cross the multiple responsibilities of the people in the group. The decision register provides a clear date and record of that decision, and exactly what was decided, if needed later.

Finally, the question often arises, "how often should we meet?" The answer lies in the primary responsibility of the group. Every group's job is to make the activities over some time period go smoothly. Hence the very common daily operations meetings that are designed to be sure everything goes well every day. Shop floor supervisors/leads usually meet weekly to coordinate activities and be sure the week goes well. The top leadership team likely meet at least monthly to review and compare financials to plans in order to make coordinated adjustments to achieve goals. The shorter the time period the group is responsible for the shorter the meetings. However, no regular meeting should exceed three hours for maximum effectiveness.

Summary

Facilitation is a skill that comes with both practice and study. These meeting management tools provide the basic guides that will allow you to immediately begin facilitating high-quality meetings between yourself and others, whether it is for one-on-one coaching of your direct reports or guiding a larger group, your meetings should become more focused, more efficient, and more effective. As you practice these skills you will also run into situations where additional facilitation methods will be valuable. These tricks of the trade such as using "go-rounds," versus "open outcry" are beyond the scope of this book, but are available on-line as needed and as you learn specifically what you are trying to do.

The primary outcomes from good facilitation are good communication and collaboration. The next chapter focuses on a model for ensuring constructive communication that helps provide a framework for the facilitation of activities.

Chapter 3
Understanding and Assessing the Parts

Using the Mobius Model as a guiding sequence, it is first valuable to come to a mutual agreement on what is currently going on in an organization to make significant improvements going forward. This assessment phase is also the first step in identifying and prioritizing areas for improvement. To accomplish this, leaders must be able to step back from the day-to-day buzz of activities and view the organization as a living breathing entity with characteristics all its own. It can be helpful to have different models for different ways to view the important parts of the organization that may need attention.

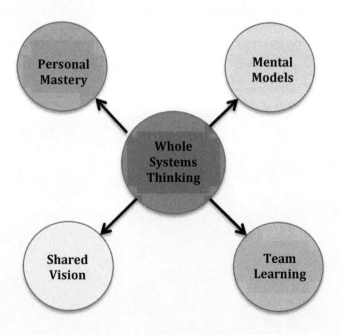

The two big areas you want to assess are:

The abilities of your people in critical areas (e.g. Fifth Discipline Model shown above)
- The effectiveness, and sufficiency, of your systems (Systems Map shown on page 30)

The Fifth Discipline Model shown above helps visualize, and is a strategic way to think about, critical aspects of the organization. It also provides a framework for communicating plans to improve.

Fifth Discipline Model
Peter Senge of MIT in his seminal book *The Fifth Discipline* suggested that highly successful companies focus on five critical areas or "disciplines." Senge found that highly successful organizations:
- View themselves as an interlaced series of systems that constantly need attention and improvement
- Recognize that a vision shared by all is critical to achieving goals
- Are constantly seeking ways to improve and develop the individual skills of all employees
- Seek opportunities for groups to learn and grow together
- Pay attention to built-in assumptions that can be limiting or supporting

He referred to these respectively as: Whole systems thinking, shared vision, personal mastery, team learning, and mental models. The image demonstrates Senge's view that Whole Systems Thinking lies at the heart of the model and is the critical to an organization's success. Senge's five disciplines act as way to organize the human aspects of the assessment process of the organization.

Successful companies have a clear and *Shared Vision* for the future. Defining and claiming a vision is the process of committing to an overarching long-term goal of an organization. Xerox CEO Anne Mulcahy credits employee alignment behind the vision as the basis of her successful and dramatic turn around of Xerox between 2001 and 2008.[15] The process for clearly defining a vision will be discussed further in Chapter 4. With a shared vision, not only are employees aware of what the organization is trying to be, but they also understand their role in achieving that vision and ultimately what's in it for them. People that share a vision have a stake in making it come to fruition.

Every individual has *Mental Models* about the organization they work for and life in general. It is important to be aware that these built-in assumptions exist and whether they are supporting of, or a limitation to, the growth and development of the organization. Hearing words like "always" or "never" in a conversation is a sure sign some form of mental model exists. Limiting mental models are often judgments of some kind, and may hide an important truth such as a fear of personal or organizational inadequacy. Mental models can be difficult to recognize because they become habitual. For example, believing you are at the whim of the economy is a very common but limiting mental model held not only by individuals, but also organizations, and even whole industries. Although economic factors have a significant impact on a business, they do not totally control one's destiny. There are, in fact, other products, other customers, and other economies that represent opportunity. A limiting mental model should not be an excuse for inaction.

At the same time there are many supporting mental models. A small organization that believes it is so responsive and flexible it can react quickly to the changing needs of its customers can be a very supportive mental model. Through the assessment process it is possible to identify existing mental models and build on those that are supporting and mitigate influence of any that are limiting.

People often learn best from each other, and an organization adopts and adapts best to change when the people are learning similar things at the same time in what is referred to as "team learning." One of the main things they must learn is how to work together. Similar to an orchestra where all the people are proficient at their various instruments but still practice as a group, individuals in a business need to practice together to make a great, united whole. An organization can enhance opportunities for success by proactively creating situations where individuals learn and grow in groups or teams, thus developing a common language for discussion and enhancing clearer communication and understanding.

An organization is as strong as the sum of its parts, and the skills of the individuals are critical to realizing future opportunity. Highly successful companies such as Google, Apple, and Amazon not only seek out the best and brightest when they are hiring, but they are continuously identifying and training staff in new skills deemed valuable to the future of both the individual and the organization. This focus on *Personal Mastery* recognizes that in today's competitive world every individual needs to get better for an organization to continue to prosper. One of the most important skills that can be developed is interpersonal communication. Interpersonal communication skills help people work well together, build relationships, and collaborate to get the most accomplished. Team learning processes discussed above foster the development of several important interpersonal communication skills such as listening and participating in dialogue.

Successful leaders recognize that an organization is a series of interconnected systems and that placing effort on optimizing the effectiveness of those systems and how they work together as a whole is of highest priority. This "whole systems thinking" approach recognizes that it is critical that leaders worry as much about how the parts and pieces of the organization go together as they do about the parts and pieces of the thing they manufacture and/or sell or the services that they provide. The ultimate measure is in how well you perform for your customers. They don't care how fast you make a certain part of the product they buy from you. All they care about is the availability, quality, performance and cost of the final product. You don't evaluate the flavor of the sausage by watching the sausage making... you taste it.

Systems Map: Whole systems thinking applied

The Oxford dictionary defines a system as *"a set of connected things or parts forming a more complex whole."* Thus an organizational system is often defined by a series of regularly connected activities. Large companies tend to have many layers of systems. Small companies need

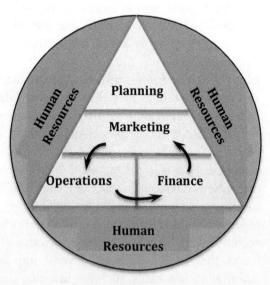

the same major systems, just fewer layers. The Systems Map

shown here provides a way of looking at the critical systems of an organization.

In this model there are five core systems that an organization must pay attention to, in the following suggested order: Planning, Marketing, Operations, Finance, and Human Resources. Each of these systems will be discussed in great detail in later chapters along with examples of the many possible subsystems within each, depending on the organization.

Every organization regardless of size has responsibility for each of these five major systems. Basically, you need to know and communicate what you are trying to do (planning), attract income to pay for your efforts (marketing), provide benefit to those providing funds (operations), measure the balance and pace of those efforts (finance) in order that you can adjust accordingly. All this rests on the critical component of having the right people doing the right things at the right time (human resources). The greater the number of employees the deeper the systems an organization needs to have.

In Chapter 1 I discussed application of the Mobius communication model to ensure good communication and as a process to solve specific conflicts or issues. In this next section and chapters 6 and 7 the use of the Mobius as a comprehensive planning tool is described.

Assessing Your Organization's Disciplines & Systems

Highly successful organizations formally assess organizational systems and performance related to the five disciplines at least annually. There are many ways to complete the assessment  process. Overall, however, the most meaningful feedback is qualitative (rather than quantitative) and the best qualitative feedback occurs in personal discussions. The absolute best information comes from confidential interviews of individuals done by people viewed as being independent of the issues. Human resources (HR) staff, if you have them, can often be viewed as independent and can complete these interviews, especially if HR is experienced with all the systems of the organization. Alternately, bringing in outside help, such as a consultant, for this part of your planning process can make a huge difference in obtaining an objective view of the organization's wants and needs. Also, organizations report an improved level of employee satisfaction and feeling of being involved in the process just by having an independent party ask them what they think!

Using the first step of the Mobius Model as a guide, your objective is to gather a wide range of perspectives on the well-being of the organization. The approach is to ask involved parties their perspective on what is (a) present that is contributing to the well-being (defined as happy and successful) of the organization and (b) what is missing, that if present would lead to a higher level of well-being. A minimum of all top leaders of the organization should be interviewed for their responses to these questions. If possible all key individuals, or individuals in key positions, should be included. You gather a list of present and a list of missing responses from as many of these individuals as possible without judging those responses.

It is common for people to have a clearer picture of what is "wrong" in certain situations rather than what is "missing." This is where the art or creative thinking comes into the

Note: the same response may occur on both Present & Missing lists due to people's different perspectives. This is normal! It just requires looking into the specifics for situations where it is missing.

questioning process in guiding the respondent to translate what is wrong into what's missing. Generally, this is accomplished by asking, "What (is missing that) would make it (whatever's wrong or whatever's good but could be better) better?"

This questioning process need not take a long time and in fact should not. Similar to financial statements, an assessment of a situation is a measure at a point in time. The longer it takes to accomplish this step the greater the variation in responses. Thus it is recommended that information be gathered over one or two days whenever possible. As discussed, personal interviews are recommended as the primary method to gather the responses, but those interviews can be supplemented by electronic surveys to broaden the input and/or gather more details about a specific item(s).

To help elicit feedback from individuals there are a number of standard questions that can be asked based on the Fifth Discipline. However, these guiding questions are meant to stimulate response from a reticent individual or elicit details about a specific issue and should be used after the individual has provided their own initial reactions to the core questions.[16] For example, guiding questions might include:

- ✓ *Is the vision of the organization clear? (If yes – then a clear vision is present. If not, then it is not).*
- ✓ *Do you have a written job description?*
- ✓ *Do you feel there is a clear plan for getting more sales?*

You will want to be sure that all five disciplines are covered and that the systems are discussed in detail consistent with the size of the organization. There are no "wrong" responses. It is fine if a person responds with an issue that is specific only to them, although it is valuable to clarify if they believe the particular issue applies to others as well. In either case, although this is an evaluation of the total organization, anything that impacts the person's view is reasonable. These inputs are not mutually exclusive and many personal issues are easily addressed.

At the end of the interviews you want each individual respondent to rank the importance of each of the items they feel are missing. That is, they rank how valuable would it be if a particular issue were improved in the next year. This is not meant to be a comparative ranking; that is you don't want them to choose between items. Often it is simplest to have the individuals rank the items from one to five, with five being "very important to address" and one being "unimportant." As a note, it is NOT uncommon for people to rank ALL their "missings" as fours or fives! They don't think of them if they are not important to them.

The next step is to list all the characteristics voiced as present by the respondents. This is a list to celebrate and areas to preserve and protect. Then the missing list can be consolidated and categorized based on the Fifth Discipline's five areas. The System Map can help organize the Whole Systems Thinking section of the responses into major subcategories. The missing categories with the highest overall rankings become potential areas to address, or *Possibilities*. That is, you want to consider the possibility that these "missings" could be present.

<u>Possibilities</u> – Next the organization must take the organized, prioritized responses, turn them into possibilities, and subsequently decide which ones can be collectively addressed over  the next year. To turn a "missing" into a "possibility" simply involves stating it in the positive. Thus, if "a clear vision

statement" is missing, then "a clear and written vision statement exists" would be the possibility. However, it is also important to acknowledge that some organizations likely have some critical, foundational components missing that are automatically the highest priority for the organization to address as soon as possible.

These are:
> A clear and shared vision (basic purpose of organization)
> Clear and agreed on values statements (basis of all HR activities)
> Clear organizational structure (who reports to whom)
> Clear roles and responsibilities for all individuals (what is each individual's priority)

Once these four items are complete they merely need to be reviewed and adjusted as needed; but, if missing, need to be put in place immediately as all other system improvements rest on this foundation. The good news is that documenting these things for existing companies is not necessarily a lengthy exercise. In fact, the first three items can often be accomplished by top leader(s) in a couple of hours and clear roles and responsibilities can be sorted out by a group in about an hour per person using the guidelines in Chapter 5.

A group meeting is a great way to value employees and communicate that an individual's input can help improve the situation for the whole.

It also models how an individual's actions are linked to the whole, setting the stage for improvement programs such as LEAN

It is valuable to report the findings and highest-ranked possibilities to <u>at least</u>[17] all the people that provided input. This is best done in person, as a group, as part of a communication strategy. This is information you want them to hear the same way at the same time. Individual input remains confidential, you only report summarized findings – often slightly reworded in the consolidation process.

At this meeting you want to do four things. You want to:
1. Answer any questions of clarification
2. Confirm that the summary fundamentally reflects what they believe to be needed (basically that their priorities made the list)
3. Inform them of the next steps that will occur as a result of their input
4. Create the time line for responding to their input and a process, including contact information, whereby they can add to their responses if they wish.

These next steps are slightly dependent on the size of the organization, its style, and the way they do planning. As a result of this meeting you primarily want to define which possibilities are proposed for consideration for the next year, define or form a team that will work on the next steps, and let each individual know their role in the future of the process (if any).

The next chapter delves into the planning system and the various types of plans that can be created depending on the size of your organization. In the succeeding three chapters official formation of the leadership team is discussed and step-by-step guidance on conducting a meeting to develop strategic and annual business plans, applicable to companies of all sizes, is provided. For best results an organization should commit one or two full days to get the basic plan in place. This approach creates the most robust plan in the shortest amount of time.

Chapter 4
Planning - Prioritizing Continuous Improvement

Chapter 3 discussed the assessment of the organization, and the organization of the assessment results into ten basic categories, including five core systems...

- Planning – how do we achieve what we want?
- Marketing – what do our customers need from us?
- Operations – how do we supply that effectively?
- Finance – how do we measure our activities?
- Human Resources – how do we organize ourselves to make it all work?

And five organizational disciplines:

- Shared Vision – how do we get everyone working on a collective goal?
- Mental Models – how do we create positive, constructive attitudes?
- Personal Mastery – how do we make every individual better at what they do?
- Team Learning – how do we make groups of people work better together?
- Whole Systems Thinking – how do we may the whole organization work more smoothly?

In this chapter the nature of the plans that apply to different uses, organization size and needs are discussed.

Why Create a Plan?

Plans are the primary communication tool of an organization. They are written declarations of what the group is trying to accomplish, and how they are going to go about achieving those objectives. Plans are also the primary way an organization defines and applies <u>whole systems thinking</u>. Plans work best when people are engaged in the formation process, either directly or through representation, and thus have buy-in to the outcome.

In this chapter the development of plans to prioritize and address the needs defined in the organizational assessment process is outlined. The assessment defined and prioritized possibilities, and the planning

Research shows that companies that write down their plans are much more successful than those that don't!

process fleshes out those possibilities, chooses those priorities that are most likely to have the biggest impact in the coming year, and for which resources are available to address. It also, creates actions, timelines, responsibilities, and benchmarks; all of these follow the sequence of the Mobius communication model.

As noted in the Introduction, this entire discussion of planning is based on the needs of people, rather than that of "things" such as processes or equipment. Experience has taught that getting everyone doing the right thing at the right time and making good timely decisions is the basis of success. Thus your plan should focus on this fundamental need. This people-centric approach does not exclude equipment or processes, quite the contrary; they are critical to some organization's success. But what it does is put people as the focus of the organization as all actions require people to make them happen. This approach is based on the idea that, when you go into a factory to show someone a machine, you have the choice of introducing the operator first and have him or her explain and demonstrate its operation of the machine or showing the machine and then saying, "Carol is the operator." Often we don't realize that is the choice we are making. I suggest choosing the former option, and making it a clear and conscious choice to put people first in all you do. Your plans should reflect that approach.

Planning Categories

There are a number of types of plans and, although language varies, it is fair to say that the following plans are most common:

- Strategic
- Business
- Marketing
- Operations
- Financial

It is clear that many plans align with the major systems of the organization. The human resource system is often the most neglected in the planning process and in reality is the most important. Organizing your staff to motivate them to achieve personal and business goals does not happen accidentally. A good plan makes it happen.

The *Planning System* is the group of activities and processes for developing, and implementing the plan; including how you will monitor and adjust activities to stay on track. This latter is the accountability component of planning.

Strategic and Annual Business Plans

In the next three chapters (Chapters 5-7) the formation of a cross-functional leadership team for your organization and the development of the associated strategic and annual business plans are discussed. Strategic plans incorporate overall strategies and objectives, which are based on the highly prioritized possibilities defined in the broad assessment of the overall well-being of the organization discussed in Chapter 3. The annual business plan includes the strategic plan plus the actions, responsibilities, and benchmarks toward achieving that plan. The annual business plan also includes budgets and projected balance sheets (these are part of the benchmarking process). More specifically:

Strategic Plans: clearly define the organization's annual and/or long-term strategies and desired outcomes or objectives. Strategic plans are cross-functional plans that seek to improve the organization as a whole. Cross-functional means you consider all systems simultaneously. Strategic plans are used to prioritize resources between major systems such as marketing and operations. Strategic plans can be very simple. In a very small organization it can be as simple as, "*this year we are going to focus our resources on improving our operating consistency*," with a goal of "*we want our gross margins to be within a 2% range of our average regardless of product or customer*." Larger companies often have at least one strategy associated with every major system. Big corporations often have strategies associated with every subsystem such as "shipping and receiving" or "inventory management." A good strategy focuses resources on the right thing needed to be successful.

Business Plan: clearly defines how you will achieve your strategies. There are short-term, generally annual, and long-term business plans, generally 3-5 years. Due to the rapidly changing nature of the world, the focus in this book is on the annual business plan. Annual business plans are also cross-functional plans, and they specifically define the annual actions, timelines, responsibilities and benchmarks for achieving overall organizational objectives based on defined strategies. Annual business plans may incorporate specific function- or system-based plans such as marketing plans, operational plans, financial plans, and human resource plans. Annual budgets and forecasted balance sheets are part of the benchmarking process in the implementation of annual plans!

Small companies may only need a broad annual business plan. In this case, it is important is to be sure it considers and addresses all the systems of the organization and includes activities to improve performance in all five disciplines. Many of these disciplines (*personal mastery, team learning, and whole systems thinking*) occur as a result of the planning process itself. But additional activities should be considered depending on the existing skillsets of people within the organization. *Alignment behind a vision* is part of the strategic planning process discussed in chapter 6, and *mental models* are addressed in both the planning process (values statements) in chapter 6 and in chapter 12 the human resources section (through clear job descriptions and conflict resolution).

Marketing, Operations, Financial and Human Resource Plans

Marketing, Operations, Financial, and Human Resource (sometimes referred to as "organizational") Plans are plans developed for the coordination of individuals within a specific system or functional area of a organization. Marketing and other system plans are needed depending on the specific organizational situation. The planning processes for these plans *occur after, and are based on*, the broader strategic and annual business plans that are developed first.

There are three dominant ways to determine IF you need a specific plan for a specific system versus just having actions within the annual plan. First, it is based on the total number of people in an organization. Small companies do not need complex plans – they just need a good written annual plan with actions that are likely very specific.

Second, it is based on the number of people within a functional area. The more people you are trying to coordinate. the more you want to agree on the details of what you are trying to do and get buy in through the planning process. System plans are especially important if you are trying to make big changes in how the organization performs in those areas.

The third indicator is the existence of a major and fairly broad annual business strategy specific to a system (e.g. *"we will grow sales by 25 percent over the next two years to customers that will value our cores skills and abilities"*). These kinds of broad strategies require a major change in activities and efforts should be carefully planned out to ensure everyone knows what you are trying to do and what is different than the previous year.

A system plan requires an additional assessment to supplement and complement the one done for the strategic plan. A system strategy defined in the strategic plan becomes the basis of this new assessment, and the leaders of that system should be the group responsible for putting together and implementing this plan. So, using the example marketing strategy above, the new assessment questions you would ask the people responsible for sales and marketing is (Mobius step #1):

What is present that would contribute to our ability to grow sales by 25 percent, and what is missing that, if it were present, would enhance our ability to achieve 25 percent growth.

Again you prioritize the missing elements based on those that you think will make the biggest difference in the coming year. The things present are those you want to preserve, with importance placed on addressing the highest priority missing elements.

Chapters 8-12 introduce the basics of these four major systems to both help you frame your assessment process for these systems and to also guide development of any specific plan you need. The leaders in the system follow the Mobius process by defining each individual's view of success for each high-priority missing (conditions of satisfaction), committing to the ones they think will make the most difference in the coming year, and then defining action steps, responsibility, and benchmarks (Mobius steps 2-6). The result is a concrete plan based on input from a variety of individuals, with guidance for implementation.

A good plan is a living, breathing document that guides the activities of the organization to achieve organizational goals. It's living and breathing to the extent that it shouldn't be stagnant. You may often adjust activities depending on changing conditions and new experiences to remain on track. The plan should be communicated as broadly as possible within the organization, and every individual should have an idea of their role in the plan and how they affect the success of the organization. Just remember, plans are like life…always forward, never straight.

Chapter 5
Forming the "Planning" Team and Preparing to Plan

Simply taking a group of individuals that collectively have a broad range of knowledge, putting them together and just doing it can be the most efficient way to create a plan. An existing leadership group can accomplish the next steps needed in the planning process or it may be necessary to formally create a group to do so. People can also be added temporarily to the team specifically for planning purposes. However, it is important that this team be formed with long-term accountability in mind. That is, at least the core of the planning team should meet regularly throughout the year to hold each other accountable to the plans they jointly agreed on!

The difference between a group and a team is that teams have:
- *Clearly defined collective goal/purpose*
- *Clear ground rules for operating*
- *Organized and structured interactions*
- *Clear means of accountability*

Why form an official "team," you ask? Isn't it more efficient if people just do their jobs and everything gets done? In a word... NO! To achieve collective[18] organizational goals requires coordination and efficient use of time. In the "old days" the way to approach this was to have the boss be the sole focus of coordination – kind of like a bee pollinating his flowers. That is, it used to be accepted that the boss would coordinate the group by meeting with each individual responsible for a functional area or system and it was his or her job to ensure that all the parts improved and contributed to the whole. The boss was also the primary source of communication between the systems. In reality, the smart boss figured out pretty quickly this was really inefficient, because when things were going well there wasn't much to talk about and when things were going poorly each individual had a different perspective (sometimes angrily) on what needed to be fixed.

Not only is the traditional approach inefficient with time, but the organization's success also relies almost exclusively on the skills of one person. In virtually all cases the collective skills and creativity of a group, including the lead person, are significantly greater than the skills and creativity of any one individual. Today, global competition moves too fast and is too complex for inefficient use of time and for any one person to have all the answers. That is why it is critical that leadership is shared in an organization, and that shared leadership is not random or left to chance. Facilitation is an important skill needed to effectively share leadership and ensure wide-ranging success. A well-facilitated leadership team is able to get more done and be more creative in finding solutions that allow the organization to compete.

To a certain extent it is simple math. Generally the boss's time is the most valuable. So, a boss can either meet with 5 direct reports one at a time for one hour each, or get much more accomplished by facilitating a meeting with all five for two hours.

In a team it is every individual's job to communicate to every other individual what is going on – e.g. what is present that is going really well and what is missing that would make their jobs go better. This is the basic function of the cross-functional team meeting. How often have you heard "we need more sales" and the sales people commenting "it's hard when our lead times are so long." This conversation needs to be direct and resolved. The Chapter on Marketing outlines how to find customers that value what you provide and how to find out what customers really want. The Operations section discusses how to provide things at lower cost, higher perceived quality, and with shorter lead times. These capabilities arise from sales and marketing leaders being part of a team talking directly to each other and for whom the collective goal is the growth and well-being of the organization.

Forming the Planning Team

It is important that a planning team be cross-functional. That is, representatives with responsibilities for the different major systems should be included to maximize coordination and for the best results. In small companies this could involve a few people with each playing several different roles. In large companies this would be more people that have specific responsibilities for an individual system. Major systems include: planning, marketing, operations, finance, and human resources (HR).

In companies with fewer than 25 employees responsibility for the major systems generally rests within two or three people. In companies of 25-60 people these five functions often rest within three or four positions. In all cases the top person is responsible for planning, and often finance as well. At 60 or more employees most companies find they need a full time HR person. The growth of the finance role is usually more dependent on the skills and interests of the top person than the number of employees. At some size (sales or number of employees) most companies do require a full time financial person.

So, the planning group should include representatives of the five core systems, at least. The addition of any other individual that is important to the organization should be considered. Generally the top person in the organization has final say on who will participate in the planning meeting and either use the facilitation skills described earlier to facilitate the meeting or outsource the facilitation to ensure desired outcomes are achieved...

The purpose of the planning or leadership team is:

> "To *define, implement, monitor and adjust activities as needed to achieve the objectives of an annual plan, the outcome of which is to significantly improve the well-being of the organization.*"

Each organization will want to reword the purpose in a way that has meaning to them, but the fundamental reason-for-being remains the same.

Getting the Team Ready for the Planning Meeting

The most efficient way to form a team and finalize the strategic portion of the plan is to simply take the group off-site and meet for a day or two. At this meeting the Mobius Model is utilized to finalize shared commitment toward achieving the objectives of a plan. The first step will be to make the team official, claim the purpose, agree on ground rules for operating together, agree on a structure for team interactions (e.g. meeting regularity and times), and agree on how accountability is going to occur (e.g. the role of this team and individuals in making decisions).

A time and place is then selected and you meet. The most efficient way to complete a plan (and most likely to actually occur) is to take the time, focus on it and get it done. In the example in the next Chapter, two days are assumed for the planning process. However, some situations may require that planning be done over a series of meetings – say half-days weekly over the course of a month. In either case, the basic things you have to accomplish are the same. The meeting space should be comfortable, interruptions should be eliminated or minimized, and all the creature comforts such as temperature, food, air quality, and noise should be addressed. Great conditions make for great plans. Studies have also shown that access to nature can lead to higher energy levels in individuals and more creative results.

Now, based on your new facilitation skills from Chapter 1 you know you need an agenda, the focus of which is defining which improvements you, as an organization, can commit to in the coming year. So the outcomes on your agenda look something like the one on the following page (with day expectations circled):

At the completion of this meeting (or meetings) you will have a true team in every sense of the word. Many companies rename this group to "leadership team," or "executive team," or "operations team." Each organization needs to evaluate their individual culture and label this team in a manner that reflects their organizational personality. Why name it? Well, simply because to communicate what is going on to everyone else in the organization you are going to have to refer to the group that is planning and managing to make things happen. So a clear and concise name is valuable.

Remember, you want to share the agenda with every individual in the planning team prior to meeting so they can prepare. In addition, IF you are meeting for 1-2 days to complete the whole process, you will want each individual to bring a document with them to the meeting (with copies to share with others) that lists the following:

- Statement of what they believe to be the primary purpose of their job.

- A list of what they see as their top 4-6 major responsibilities.

- An estimate of the percent of their annual time they think they should be spending on each responsibility.

> *A major responsibility can be defined as a group of related tasks for which the total time you spend annually is greater than 5 percent.*

In addition, the top leader should bring written statements of the organization's vision, mission and organizational values, if they already exist. If they do not, as is most common, then the top leader should bring a draft of a vision statement for finalization. In addition, the top leader should bring copies of the organizational chart to share.

Now, you are ready to meet and finalize the plan. The next two discuss the planning meeting. Vision, Mission, and Values Statements are also discussed in great detail.

1) Check-in: (How are you? Anything in the way of being fully present?)
2) Review of Agenda Items: In this case the team forming and planning process defines the sequence of agenda items.
3) The purpose of group is finalized and agreed to
4) Ground rules for meeting together are defined and committed to (and will be used in current meeting)
5) A clear and agreed on *Vision* statement exists
6) A clear and agreed on *Mission* statement exists
7) Clear and agreed on *Values* Statements are in place
8) A clear organizational *Structure* exists
9) *COS* are in place for each prioritized *Possibility* defined by the assessment
10) There is clear agreement and commitment to organizational improvement *Strategies¹* for the coming year
11) Clear *Roles & Responsibilities* are in place for each individual in planning group
12) *Next Steps* are in place for refining the Actions required to meet each condition of satisfaction
13) Clear *Responsibility* for championing each condition of satisfaction is in place
14) *Recognition* activities and dates are clearly defined and agreed on (benchmarking & celebration)
15) *Review of Action-Decision Register*
16) *Checkout (What was present that made it a successful meeting and what was missing that would have made it better)*

Other Outcomes

Team Learning – Greater understanding of self and others as team members occurs, Greater understanding of organization occurs

Personal Mastery – Meeting management skills are modeled, Control dramas are discussed, Communication skills are practiced, and Collaboration is modeled

Chapter 6
The Planning Meeting – Day One

With a comfortable site, good food planned and no distractions, the groundwork has been laid. Ideally you have set aside at least one full day and ideally two. You will want large poster pad type paper (e.g. Post-it versions) that you use can capture results and to aid with clarification of language. Either the facilitator documents information on these or you need someone else to "scribe." Now the meeting begins.

Check-in Process:
To check in, everyone answers the questions: How are you? Is there anything in the way of your being here? What were your best and worst team experiences previously and why?

You want to capture on the post-it paper the "value" that made their experiences good or bad. For example, if people report people were always late at or spent lots of effort talking but getting nowhere then the missing value might be "reliability" or "respect" or "timeliness." You should specifically clarify with the person what specific value they thought was missing. Accumulate this for use in the Values discussion.

Finalize the Purpose of Team:
As noted in Chapter 4, in general the purpose of the top leadership team (or planning team) is to:

"To define, implement, monitor and adjust activities as needed to achieve the objectives of an annual plan, the outcome of which is to significantly improve the well-being of the organization and its people."

It is at this point you reword this as needed to fit the culture and specific needs of your organization. The goal of

49

this process is to explore what people interpret as being meant by each part of the purpose, as ultimately you want everyone to agree on the basic meaning and commit to the purpose. Do NOT get hung up on detailed wordsmithery. At some point good enough is good enough and you can come back to specific details later if needed. You are primarily after agreement with the gist of the purpose and commitment to it. Generally this process should take about 30 minutes. It can be helpful, and helps speed the process if top leaders prepare and propose a purpose to start the discussion.

Agree to Ground Rules

Ground rules were introduced in the Facilitation section in Chapter 1, and many of the examples there make sense for almost all teams. At this meeting you simply need to claim 5-10 that are the highest priorities for you as a group. This is a discussion that should be inclusive and robust, but need not be lengthy. It doesn't have to be perfect; it just has to be a significant clarification from the past. Generally, this process takes 30 minutes to one hour.

Next you want to clarify Vision, Mission and Values. This part is critically important and, if missing, is the basis of most problems in organizations. Thus I will spend significant time discussing these tools. If you already have clear and agreed on Vision/Mission and Values Statements then you can skip ahead – although you still might find the following discussion valuable.

Creating a Shared Vision...

(If you don't know where you're going, any path will get you there!)
Today companies trying to navigate the stormy seas of competitive markets are facing extraordinary rates of change. Drive-thru expectations have met Internet access and

combined to generate customers that are well informed, demanding, and have unlimited options. Organizations that succeed in the face of these winds of change are finding that a clear organizational vision is the anchor that keeps their organization from drifting into oblivion. *A clear Vision is the most important component of an organization's plan*; yet often the most neglected and misunderstood.

It isn't only for-profit businesses that are guilty of this neglect. Government agencies, non-profits, and universities struggle with this same issue. Organizations of all kinds rarely take the time to ask themselves the fundamental question "why do we exist?" Or if they do ask, the answer is defined so broadly that almost any solution fits. Sometimes, organizational leaders rationalize the lack of attention to vision, saying that the "situation or the market requires us to be broad and flexible." As I noted in Chapter 1, a lack of a vision is a failure to commit; it is a failure to choose, prioritize, and stay focused, which often leads to a decline in organizational effectiveness. A lack of clear vision can also lead to someone else prioritizing your efforts for you.

Vision and Change

One of the greatest stresses created by competitive forces is that placed on an organization's vision. For example, an organization that has prided itself for years as being the most efficient, lowest cost producer of chairs for the educational market suddenly faces foreign competition that is not simply cheaper, but a great deal cheaper (perhaps 25-50 percent less expensive)! This competition not only threatens the profits of the organization, but it is also a threat to the very nature of all that the organization represents. Too often organizational leaders facing such pressures place all of their efforts on the operational side, trying to produce ever cheaper products, or on the marketing side in trying to find new markets, without first placing the effort where it needs to be – on reviewing the organization's vision. This is not to say that an organization must necessarily change its vision in the face of new market conditions, but it is critically important to recognize that collective efforts and strategies are largely driven by who the organization believes it is or wants to be and that future decisions should be conscious of this choice. Competitive pressures MAY require a substantial change in the organizational vision.

In the heat of the battle small things can become major issues. In the above example, leaders might consider whether "the organization is a wood products manufacturer that makes chairs, or a chair manufacturer that uses wood?" Just making that simple clarification in vision can have enormous impact on future decisions, and on how the organization is viewed by its current and potential customers.

It is also important to recognize that sometimes a change in vision is essential for growth, or even survival. When the pressures are such that an organization feels the need to "do" something dramatically different, it is usually an indication that a review of the vision is the place to start.

It is generally true that any new vision should be developed with broad stakeholder participation – i.e. by infusing new blood into the organization. The same individuals that have held tightly to the existing vision are unlikely to easily envision major changes or the breadth of possibilities that truly exist. Increased diversity is valuable, whether in the form of race, gender, background, or simply functional responsibility. In general, the greater the diversity and the greater the creativity the broader the options that emerge as a result. The cross-functional team is a form of structured organizational diversity and increases the potential for alignment of individuals and systems.

The Vision Statement

The American Collegiate Dictionary defines vision as "a mental view or image." To an organization, the vision is both a picture of what those within an organization expect that organization to look like in the future and a reflection of what those people view as the organization's daily priorities. To the extent those two images are clear, and processes for effecting change well established, the result is quite likely a well-oiled machine. To the extent that they differ, or are unclear, the organization is likely to struggle.

Visions can be lofty. For example, in May 1961 President John F. Kennedy delivered a stirring speech that set the agenda for the U.S. space program. He surprised the nation by declaring that by the end of the decade the United States would "…send a man to the moon and return him safely to earth." With this simple phrase, JFK provided the "vision" for NASA for the 1960s.

The State of Maine committed to a vision of being a leader in certified forestland and certified products. Their specific goals are to:

- *Certify 10 million acres in the state by the end of 2007*
- *Increase the volume of wood from certified sources to 60 percent of the statewide total by the end of 2009.*

The President's vision was also highly functional in that it became possible, given both the goal and the timeframe, for NASA teams to define the intermediate steps necessary to achieve the ultimate goal. As a result, the broad vision framed the basis for many, many narrower, decisions.

All organizations, whether public or private, large or small, young or old, for-profit or not-for-profit, should have in place a clearly articulated a vision for their future desired state. In general, the vision statement should announce where as an organization you want to go -- to the moon for example! -- Or paint a broad picture of what you want the organization to become.

Vision statements do not need to be, and should not be lengthy—a phrase or two is sufficient. A written vision statement is a compass that guides everyone in the organization in understanding the degree to what he or she is doing is furthering the future of the organization. Even a company with only three employees cannot afford to have them operate in a vacuum with no idea where the organization is going. Day-to-day supervision is not enough.

The ultimate evaluation of the clarity of a vision comes in the form of what is sometimes referred to as the "cocktail party test." If you can explain your vision in one sentence to a stranger at a cocktail party, and they can repeat it back to you in their own words, you have a clear vision. If you can't, or they can't, then it isn't as clear as you might think it is.

Vision statements should include the following information:
- ➢ What the organization wants to be
- ➢ Concepts for future products or services (not specific products and services)
- ➢ Some additional structure for decision making (e.g. timeframes, behavior guidelines, or competitive approach)

We want to be ...

The leaders of an organization typically develop vision statements, often with input from stakeholders. Leadership is responsible for creating a vision that puts into words a view of a realistic, credible, attractive future for the organization— a condition that is better in some important ways than what currently exists. It also should describe the fundamental approach to achieving that vision.

54

Beware of generic statements such, "we want to be the best in the business" without some form of qualitative description. Phrases such as most reliable, most responsive, most creative, are all better descriptors of a organization's desires than "best." And don't be afraid to think big, if that is what you really want. A failure to state that you want to be the largest wood flooring manufacturer in the region, when that is what you really hope to achieve means that others within the organization will likely be accepting of a lower goal than otherwise might be possible. Always remember the old adage, "think, speak, and do." Vision is about speaking your hopes and dreams, in order to get the whole organization working to the same end. Organizations that can't speak about their dreams, rarely achieve them.

We want to...

A vision statement presents an opportunity to be motivational. Statements like, "we want to double in size," are motivational only to the extent individuals interpret that as a benefit to them. A better motivation is to directly address why you want to double in size, e.g. to increase opportunities for employment, create a more stable organization, or provide benefits to all. Remember, in general, stakeholders will always look to the vision to identify what is in it for them. A good example is Cirrus airplanes, whose vision is to manufacture the safest airplane in the industry. The result is their planes are unique in that they have parachutes, they attract employees from all over the country who are excited about their creative approach, and they have a long list of customers for whom safety and creativity are a priority.

A vision should be clarifying, but general enough that it allows for flexibility and creativity. A rather famous article by Theodore Levitt, called Marketing Myopia[19], discussed the failure of organizations to describe themselves broadly enough. In one example Levitt suggested that the struggle of the railroad industry was due primarily to the fact that they described themselves as being in the "railroad" business, rather than in the transportation business. Thus, even though needs for transportation of people and freight increased significantly over the years, railroads failed to benefit from that growth.

Visioning is also about __making__ decisions: What are the criteria for defining what is essential for doing business?

Research has shown that businesses generally separate themselves, and compete in, three areas: price, innovation, and customer service (similar to Porter's Model). [20] For example, these three core approaches can be summarized in the following way:

- Price -- strive to become the lowest cost producer, (example: commodity product manufacturers such as steel or lumber)
- Innovation -- invest in creative processes, technology and new product development, (example: 3M) and
- Customer service -- focus on developing an intimate understanding of the customer and being willing to do almost anything to make the customer happy, regardless of cost. (Example: Nordstrom, a department store famous for its employees running to other stores to get items their customers want but that Nordstrom doesn't carry)

Deciding the core approach is both among the most important decisions an organization can make, and generally the most controversial in discussion – because, in truth, all of the above traits are critical. However, the clarity of vision can be evaluated based on the ability of the front line employee to make independent decisions. If the core approach is clear, front line employees instinctually know what to do in most situations.

And, yes, customer service focused and innovative organizations must be cost-effective! And low-cost producers must still provide a high level of customer service! However, it is important to recognize that decisions are being made every day on everything from capital investment, to staffing, to product or service characteristics based on leadership's core choice of approach. The clearer the "core approach" is from a vision point of view the more consistent and effective the organization will be.

The time it takes to create alignment behind a vision is based on the preparation of the leader. That is why it is suggested that the top leader bring a draft to the meeting. In fact, in the top leader's eyes the draft statement may be considered complete when they bring it. The role of the team is to ask questions of clarification, suggest additions or deletions, and to suggest, if necessary, slightly different language that may be more motivating even though it may have essentially the same meaning. Assuming the top leader brings a fairly complete "draft" the process of clarifying and committing to the vision should only take about one hour.

5) Clarifying and Agreeing on the Mission
Although often used interchangeably, Vision and Mission can actually be interpreted quite differently. Technically, mission is defined as "a task or job someone or group is given to do" (Merriam Webster). The Oxford Dictionary defines the Mission Statement as "the formal summary of the aims and values of the company, organization or individual." So the Mission of the organization can either be broader or narrower than the Vision Statement (or the same) depending on interpretation. However, leaving a Mission open for interpretation is not

good communication. It really it doesn't matter which term, Vision or Mission, is used as long as all employees know what it means. Certain groups such as religious organizations and some kinds of nonprofits find the term Mission more appealing.

However, I have personally found it valuable to use the Mission Statement as a way to build on the Vision Statement and further clarify the direction of the organization. That is, to create a Mission Statement from a Vision Statement, I have simply added the market focus of the organization. So if your vision is, "to be the most innovative manufacturer of custom cabinets in Kentucky," then your mission might be:

"To be the most innovative manufacturer of custom cabinets supplying high-end builders in Kentucky."

The Mission in this use further clarifies and focuses the activities of the marketing systems of the organization. It doesn't mean you won't sell to people outside of Kentucky or to people other than builders in Kentucky. It simply means that is where your focus and investments in marketing will occur. Used this way a Mission statement can be a valuable strategic addition to your broader Vision Statement, but it is not necessary. There are other ways to focus your marketing depending on the nature and size of your organization.

Clarifying and Committing to core Values Statements[21]
Values Statements are the most important and the most neglected organizational guidelines you can have. Put simply, Values Statements define the way everyone is expected and agrees to behave within an organization. They are the tool for correcting misbehavior and rewarding good. All employees should formally commit to the Values Statements. Many companies have employees sign a written agreement based on these and other statements each year.

What are Values Statements?

The Oxford Dictionary defines Value as the importance, worth or usefulness of something. Values are those things that are important to someone. Thus, Values statements clarify the aspects of interpersonal relationships that an organization feels are important, and explicitly define how people will behave with each other in the organization and with their customers, suppliers, and in the community. Herein I recommend that you create a short list of individual and high priority values statements rather than a summary descriptive paragraph. I have found the list version simpler to understand by all employees and specific enough to use in rewarding or remonstrating behavior.

Why are values statements neglected? Many leaders feel values statements are unnecessary. They suggest that individuals "know" how to behave. It is true that most of us tend to assume that others think the same way about the world as we do. However, what a person views as being *respectful* behavior, for example can vary greatly by culture, ethnicity, and upbringing; and the challenge is there are literally hundreds of terms for different values in the English language. Each has its own nuance. Being clear about those values that your organization believes to be important and what they mean to you can make a big difference in building strong relationships, attracting and hiring the right people, and fostering constructive behavior.

> *Your Values Statements are an opportunity to clarify your commitment to environment and society. For example, by stating categorically, "We value business practices that support a sustainable environment" you are creating the base from which all stakeholders can begin challenging and improving the organization's environmental impact.*

Some example Values statements include, we value:

- Respect for each other and ourselves
- Trust in each other
- Timeliness in all things
- Creativity

In general, "quality" is NOT a value, as quality has no common definition in the business world. So if you view quality as a valuable, then you need to be more specific about exactly what it is about quality you prioritize, e.g. responsiveness, or proactivity if you are talking about service, or it might be durability or individual craftsmanship if you are talking more about the product.

Also the things you claim as values are the things you will prioritize in activities to support. For example, a design firm may have creativity as an organizational value, and thus it would make sense that they would then put effort into activities that train or inspire creative thinking. Unique office spaces, seating arrangements, use of games and toys are all examples of practices that attract and retain creative people.

Some Important value statements
Although each organization needs to sort out their own priority list of values based on who they are and the way they like to operate, there are four specific value statements that are suggested here because they are specifically useful in constructively resolving interpersonal behavior issues. These values are based on those identified by Angeles Arrien, PhD in her book the Four-Fold Way.[22]

Arrien was a cultural anthropologist that researched human behavior globally and found some interesting characteristics that are useful to businesses. Arrien discovered that regardless of where you are in the world there are four archetypes (footprints, models, paradigms) for how people interact with others, particularly under stress, and that our dominant approach is pretty well ingrained into us by the time we are toddlers. James Redfield, in his book "The Celestine Prophecy [23]" referred to these interactions as "control dramas" and recognized that each of the four archetypes had a positive constructive characteristic, a shadow or control drama component, and an associated relationship value. These four archetypes she labeled as the warrior, the healer, the teacher, and the visionary as they are recognized and described in indigenous cultures globally. The four-fold way and control dramas will be discussed in greater detail in the human resources section, but here the values are important and relevant. The four values are:

- Showing up and being fully present
- Paying attention to what has heart and meaning
- Non-attachment to an outcome and being open to possibilities
- Speaking the truth without blame or judgment

In this context, "showing up" as a value is that you want people to show up to work, to meetings to everything the organization does fully present, i.e. physically, emotionally, intellectually, and spiritually.

"Paying attention to what has heart and meaning" means that you want people to bring both their passion and caring to work. If you can link what matters to individuals to what matters to the organization you have an unbeatable combination.

Being nonattached to an outcome (& open to possibilities) is concerned with people engaging with others without being already committed to one solution. This nonattachment leaves the individual open to the possibility that others input might create a more complete and higher quality solution through collaboration. The nonattachment value also recognizes that organizations need to change and evolve constantly, and that the people within them need do so as well. Thus people need to be open to new and different ideas, ways of doing things, and ways of thinking.

Four-Fold Way

Healer	Teacher
Pays Attention to what has Heart & Meaning	Nonattached to an Outcome
"Celebrates Individuals"	*"Asks enlightening questions"*
Control Drama: Victim	Control Drama: Interrogator

Visionary	Warrior
Speaks the truth without blame or judgment	Shows up fully engaged
"Creates possibilities"	*"Makes compelling invitations"*
Control Drama: Aloof	Control Drama: Intimidator

Based on the work of Angeles Arrien, PhD and James Redfield

Speaking the truth without blame or judgment recognizes that being caring and direct is a much more successful way for people to operate in an organization than to try to do things indirectly or manipulatively. A discussion of individual judgments can also be a guide for understanding the truth about what's going on. This value also recognizes the responsibility of every individual to speak out and take responsibility for things they see or hear, and not to be passive bystanders. It is the basis for everyone taking responsibility for improvement.

These four values identified by Angeles Arrien are suggested as valuable additions to your list of Value Statements as they are the most commonly used in helping people to work better together and build strong relationships.

A list of Values Statements that the team can agree on is generally longer the first time this list is generated than it will eventually end up, as over time people find terms that encompass multiple statements in ways meaningful to all. It is better to be too long and too detailed the first time, and inclusive of everyone's opinions than to try to be too precise. You want everyone to agree on and support the list... and commit to what it portrays.

Clear Vision, Mission, and Values Statements should last for years with, perhaps, some tweaking. It is critical that they are clear, motivational, and guide important decisions.

Clearly defined organizational structure

The next step in organizing for success is defining the organizational structure. Although surveys suggest most people believe an organizational structure is a standardized thing, most companies actually implement them differently. Thus the structure tells you a lot about an organization. As discussed previously, there are two primary ways of creating an organizational structure; one based on a traditional hierarchal structure with the boss overseeing independent individuals working in silos and the boss doing all the intermediate coordination and

A great interview question, is to ask a person to draw their organizational structure of who reports to whom and why at their current or past place of work. You will learn a lot about how that person thinks, how they see organizations, and what they know.

63

communication. The second approach is based on a system of teams. This book focuses on the team approach as a way to enhance communication and organizational success.

The top leader should bring to the planning meeting an illustration of the organizational structure of your organization. Ultimately you want this chart based on positions rather than people, but a first draft can be focused on the people as the positions currently stand. Experience tells us that most companies, and especially small ones, have a hard time with this process, specifically when it comes to who reports to whom. I often find that some people have multiple "bosses" and exactly who is responsible for what is unclear. The organizational chart exercise is the opportunity to clarify this. If you assume that leaders are responsible for the growth and development of their direct reports, than this is a way to frame the chart. Who is responsible for the growth and development of each individual in the organization – and NO indirect links allowed!! You can have dotted lines if you are a hierarchal organization, but no person can have two bosses!!

The discussion about structure can often be lively and challenging; but often equally enlightening. For many organizations it resolves long held issues. The resolution may not be perfect, but it will be clear for the first time and with clarity comes the chance that a perfect (or far better) solution will eventually be achieved.

Some Guidelines for Creating Structure
There are a couple of methods or "rules of thumb" linked to the structure of an organization that have proven to be extremely valuable in supporting clear communication. These are:

- Rule of seven
- Time theory of management

Rule of Seven

The rule of seven is simply a guideline that suggests that humans, by and of their very nature, can only prioritize a small number of options; and good decision-making is about prioritizing between choices. Experience and some research suggest that maximum effective number is seven. As an example, consider when you are asked to prioritize responses to a marketing survey. Generally, when you are asked to choose between two choices it is easy. If you are asked to prioritize a series of three options (that is pick what to do first, second, and third) it is still fairly easy for most people. However, as you add choices, most people start to have significant difficulty picking between options when you have more than five choices; and very few people can prioritize between more than seven things. What you find is that you begin to group them (e.g. top 3, bottom 3 and one in the middle) so that people tend to actually have 3, 4 or 5 priorities with more than 7 things. It is simply how our brains work. It is for this reason most good marketing surveys ask you to rank no more than five options.

Thus the same is true with dealing with people. So the rule of seven is simply, "no individual should have to prioritize more than seven areas of responsibility – including people." This also means fewer is better. So ideally, no one has more than seven direct reports. But "wait," you say, "I only have 25 employees… I don't need four bosses." All we're saying is that if you have ten direct reports, for example as head of operations for a small company, the company is better off if you give someone a "lead" or similar responsibility for assisting with three of those individuals than it is having you try to pay attention to all ten. Someone and some things will get shortchanged. The people will get more attention (more training and development) and the details are more likely to be better taken care of with few priorities. But always remember, the *Rule of Seven* is a handy guideline, not a law.

Time Theory of Management

The second rule of thumb suggests that one easy way to divide up and manage responsibilities in a company is by time. That is, everyone within an organization should be responsible for all activities within a time period and all activities have some time schedule to them. As an example, consider a manufacturing company with 75 total employees. The time guidelines might look something like this:

> *Time Theory of Management follows the Rule of Seven as well! In general there is no need to have more than 7 leadership levels in an organization!*

- <u>President</u> – responsible for ensuring the company is ready for next year
- <u>Operations manager</u> – responsible that the company is ready for next month
- <u>Shop Supervisors</u> – responsible for ensuring that the company is ready for next week
- <u>Shop Leads</u> – responsible for ensuring the organization is ready for tomorrow
- <u>Shop floor individuals</u> – responsible for making sure that everything happens during the day that is supposed to happen

So you can see from this model, the job of everyone except the individuals that actually make stuff is successively and successfully getting ready to make it happen. People like salesmen fit into this schedule as well, defined by the lead times involved. So if you have a three-week lead-time the salesman is dominantly responsible for getting business for next month, similar to the operations manager. Similarly, depending on the company and its specific needs, the human resources person could be supporting either the operations manager (finding employees for next month) or the supervisors. The basic idea is that everyone except the people that are selling or making something is responsible for getting ready for that process to happen.

A benefit to this approach is that you can tell when things are going to go "off track" in advance of when it actually will happen by watching out for when individuals shrink their time scale activities too far. It is always appropriate, and often necessary for individuals to shift one time level in the process to be able to monitor what's going on and to flex to changing needs. However, if, for example you see the shop floor supervisor, or a sales person from the above example, operating manufacturing equipment on the shop floor you know that next month's resources (sales, inventory, sufficient personnel, etc.) are in danger of being missing.

It also helps define the chain of command. If a shop floor employee has a concern that needs to be addressed immediately (e.g. is this product coming out of the machine acceptable) they should have all the tools and information to make that decision. On the other hand, if they see something that might improve the situation at some future date, they would talk to the person responsible for making changes on that time-scale such as the lead or supervisor. This also works in reverse. As an example, if an employee goes to the CEO and says "I think this piece of equipment is making a poor quality product," the CEO has to recognize whether or not this is a capital issue (e.g. later this year or next year and his responsibility) or a maintenance issue (shop supervisor or operations manager's responsibility) or simply a current decision that the employee or his/her lead should have the training to address. Even though we tend to want to give answers as leaders, to sound knowledgeable, caring and involved, recognizing our ideas may be out of scale for the issue is critical to eliminating potential time wasting, and perhaps misdirected, activities.

A team-based organizational chart looks like a hierarchal structure with a team overlay as shown in figure below.

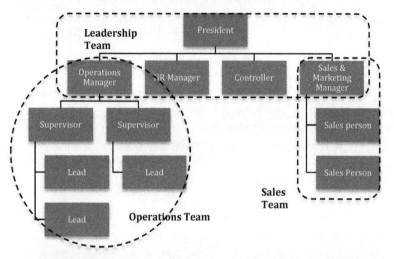

The leadership team shown is a "cross-functional" team, made up of individuals operating on the same or similar time scale and representing different functions or systems. In contrast, the operations and sales teams are "functional teams" representing individuals from two major systems of the organization.

Each of these teams is also working at a different time scale. That is, the leadership team primarily focuses on making the year be successful and thus is monitoring and adjusting activities on a monthly (usually) or quarterly basis. The operations team is generally aimed at making each month successful, and monitors and adjusts weekly to make everything happen successfully. The marketing team varies greatly by organization. But in most organizations it is fair to say that even though marketing works on an annual plan, the focus of most marketing teams is to make each quarter successful, with constant monitoring and adjustments monthly to make this happen. Finally, similar to the operations team the financial group is focused on monthly reporting (to banks, governments, owners, and the other teams) with monitoring and adjustments weekly (payroll, Accounts Receivable, etc) to optimize the monthly reports. In all cases "monitoring and adjusting" assumes these are minimum meeting schedules.

Once clear and agreed on Vision, Mission, Values, and Structure have been attained it is important to communicate these to the balance of the organization. Communicating these should be part of the action plan to be developed later.

Conditions of Satisfaction are in Place for each Highly-Prioritized Possibility From the Assessment

It is important to define what success would look like for each of the highest priority "possibilities" that were defined in the assessment. Experience suggests that a large number of  these have been addressed by the above steps. You should have five to seven major possibilities left to discuss. For each of these possibilities you want to define success. It is helpful to use the term "Conditions of Satisfaction (COS) for this process, because at the end of defining these requirements you will ask each individual *"if we met this list of conditions, would you agree that we succeeded in addressing this possibility for the year?"*

To define these COS you simply take each possibility and ask the question "how would I know we succeeded?" and get every individual's input. As noted earlier, some possibilities might need only one or two COS to make everyone happy. Some might have 5-10. It depends on how much these possibilities affect individuals across systems. Remember a condition of satisfaction is important even if only one person cares about it. For example one person might really care about the timing of something whereas this might not matter to everyone else. As long as the condition does not directly conflict with others needs the condition should be considered. However, ultimately all team members should support the inclusion of each COS. Conditions are detailed and should have dates attached as needed. Example condition of satisfaction statements for the purchase of a piece of new equipment might be:

- The cost of the new equipment does not exceed $25 thousand including installation.
- The piece of equipment is installed by April 30th, prior to our busy season.
- The piece of equipment only takes up 100 square feet of floor space in the warehouse.
- An operator is trained prior to installation and participates in installation to enhance understanding of equipment.
- The operator is one of the individuals displaced by our LEAN activities in the XYZ department.
- Data is in place before and after installation to determine equipment's impact on efficiencies and net product cost.

Notice the wording is important and should be clarified with each individual to be sure what they meant is captured accurately.

This process can take quite a while to go through all 5-7 possibilities. On average it takes about 45 minutes per possibility for a group of 5-10 leaders.

A note of caution here – many people are reluctant to commit to possibilities until they know what actions are going to be taken, and thus include activities as conditions of satisfaction. It is important to focus on outcomes, rather than activities at this point in the process and not limit the options. Effectively you are saying "these outcomes important even if we don't know how to achieve them yet."

There is Clear agreement on Improvement Strategies for the year

Once all the COS are in place for all possibilities, you know what you are committing to. So now is the time you vote on which possibilities you have the resources to complete in the next  year. As noted here this should not be a passive vote. Each person should affirm their support, or not, for each individual possibility. In some cases you might find that a person does not support working on it because you missed a condition of satisfaction, which you can add at this time. For example, in the example above when it comes to voting, the head of operations might add the condition that the "maintenance staff installation support time limited to the equivalent of one day."

The "possibilities" with COS that you agree on become your strategies for the next year. Effectively you now have a strategic plan!

This is a great stopping point to end the "meat" of day one. Experience suggests that there is also a great opportunity for team building by having the group go to dinner together and discuss informally the day's activities and accomplishments.

At this point you should have a wall (or walls) covered with sticky poster paper of the days accomplishments. Preferably you want to leave these up for reference on day two, but if this is not possible you certainly want to document all the information and share it with all participants.

Now you want to check-out from day one, asking the questions, "what was present that made this a successful day" and "what was missing that would have made this a better day?" Be open to specific and important details such as:

- Didn't like the location (or loved it)
- Wanted more time for team-building
- Food was great!
- Would have liked to go for walk at noon (it's a lot of sitting for some people)
- The facilitation was really helpful

By documenting this feedback you can continually improve the process. The figure below provides some example strategies for each major system, and the next chapter discusses day two of the planning meeting.

Example agreed-on Strategies (for the next 12 months)
  The <u>Strategic Plan</u> would include the COS for each strategy

<u>Planning</u>: We will communicate our plans and our performance toward them, monthly, to all employees.

<u>Operations</u>: We will focus operational efforts on reducing our reaction times (including lead times) by 20 percent.

<u>Marketing</u>: We will focus marketing efforts on identifying and attracting an experienced sales person that can bring additional business in his/her first year.

<u>Human Resources</u>: We will implement a semiannual, constructive, performance review process.

<u>Finance</u>: We will create a costing system that compares costs by customer and by product.

<u>Finance</u>: We will create a 12-month rolling forecasting/budgeting system.

MEETING AGENDA - OUTCOMES

1) Check-in: (How are you? Anything in the way of being fully present?)
2) Review of Agenda Items: In this case the team forming and planning process defines the sequence agenda items.
3) The purpose of group is finalized and agreed to
4) Ground rules for meeting together are defined and committed to (and will be used in current meeting)
5) A clear and agreed on *Vision* statement exists
6) A clear and agreed on *Mission* statement exists
7) Clear and agreed on *Values* Statements are in place
8) A clear organizational *Structure* exists
9) *COS* are in place for each prioritized *Possibility* defined by the assessment
10) There is clear agreement and commitment to organizational improvement *Strategies*[1] for the coming

Day 2 year
11) Clear *Roles & Responsibilities* are in place for each individual in planning group
12) *Next Steps* are in place for refining the Actions required to meet each condition of satisfaction
13) Clear *Responsibility* for championing each condition of satisfaction is in place
14) *Recognition* activities and dates are clearly defined and agreed on (benchmarking & celebration)
15) *Review of Action-Decision Register*
16) *Checkout (What was present that made it a successful meeting and what was missing that would have made it better)*

Other Outcomes

- <u>Team Learning</u> – Greater understanding of self and others as team members occurs, Greater understanding of organization occurs
- <u>Personal Mastery</u> – Meeting management skills are modeled, Control dramas are discussed, Communication skills are practiced, and Collaboration is modeled.

Chapter 7
The Planning Meeting – Day Two

At the close of day the team committed to a series of strategies, each with a number of COS attached. As noted in Chapter 3, experience and research suggest that the first major assessment of an organization tends to find four major missing elements. These are:

- Alignment behind the *Vision* and/or Mission
- Clear and agreed on *Values*
- Clear and agreed on Organizational *Structure*
- Clear and agreed on roles and *Responsibilities* for all leaders
- Clear and agreed on ground rules for operating together

On day one the process of addressing the *Vision*, *Values* and *Structure* was begun. All that's left on those three items is to communicate them to the rest of the organization. If your organization already had these things in place, in writing, then the time spent planning on day one can be reduced. There is still value in reviewing and formally agreeing to these things. But if they are in place they can usually be reviewed and agreed to as still appropriate or adjusted accordingly in less time than it takes to create and come to agreement on them the first time.

On day two the process of generating Action items/next steps, defining Clear Responsibilities (or Champions), and *Recognition* or Benchmarking timelines begins.

The Action Plan
As noted previously, most leaders today are experts at creating action plans and are taught independent problem

solving from an early age. But the truth is that while this problem solving approach may be fine for very simple and unimportant issues, it is seldom effective for dealing with more complex issues such as defining how to make major change within an organization and the collaborative creation of business plans. 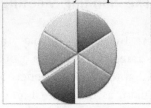 One facet of the independent problem-solving approach is that it tends to be highly iterative (meaning you keep working on aspects of the same problem for years), and lacking in group input and support. In reality the problem solving is linear - the Mobius approach can be both linear and systemic. To a certain extent the Mobius model follows the old adage, "measure twice… cut once."

The heart of an action plan is the generation of a list of the <u>major</u> actions that will address each condition of satisfaction (hereafter COS). Some COS are very straightforward and require only one action item to accomplish them. Others may take up to five action items to put them in place. You don't want more than five action items for a strategy if you can avoid it. If you are getting more than this you are probably getting too detailed.

There is a sequence to how you assign action items. It is best to do all marketing items first; operations second, finance third, and human resources last. It is at this point that completion dates are assigned to all major action items. You do not want to assign responsibilities as yet. That is the next and separate step in the process. Remember, the strategies you have developed are based on the possibilities you created out of the highly prioritized missings defined in the assessment process. Just because a particular system does not have a lot of high priority needs does not mean it is not important – it simply means there are higher priority things to focus on in the coming year.

Developing an action plan can appear to be a fairly tedious process, but is really not that time consuming if done at the beginning of the second day and then put aside.

Clear Responsibilities

In the Mobius Model assigning responsibility is the fifth step in the process. This is unusual, as most organizations tend to assign responsibility at the idea or possibility stage. However, experience shows that organizations that assign responsibility at the Possibility stage (i.e. it was Sarah's idea, she should champion it) results over time in less ideas for improvement being generated, as bright busy people do not suggest additional things to do that they believe they have insufficient  time to take on. In addition, you have not determined the major tasks yet, so you want to be sure the individual that is responsible has the skills needed to take on the tasks.

Once action items have been identified, it is known what skills are needed, providing a firmer basis for assigning responsibility. As noted earlier, major responsibilities of the leaders (and others) are often missings identified in the assessment process. Thus this issue must first be addressed before specifically assigning and agreeing to specific new actions. To facilitate this process a type of job description is recommended that is designed to have:

- Clear expectations
- Clear agreement
- Clear outcomes

The performance review process will be discussed in Chapter 10, but is based on the Mobius Model and designed to be direct, highly constructive and supportive rather than confrontational. Thus the Job Description incorporates language from the Mobius Model, and will appear similar in many ways to the planning process.

> *Consistency in language facilitates good communication!*

Each Job Description should have five components. These are:
1. Purpose of the position
2. Major responsibilities
3. Percentage of time expected annually on each responsibility
4. COS[24] for each responsibility
5. Major tasks to meet each COS

It should be possible to complete and agree to parts one through four by both the individual and the group during day two of the planning meeting. Part five can be completed by the individual and presented at a later date.

Many companies have job descriptions based almost exclusively on tasks, and in truth tasks are extremely important. However I have found that holding a person responsible for outcomes is more fruitful than trying to monitor and evaluate the relative importance and performance of individual tasks. This outcome-based approach allows for the grouping of tasks into more general responsibilities. A major responsibility can be defined as any related group of

> *Major Responsibility: Any group of related tasks that combined take more than 5 percent of a person's time annually.*

tasks that, in total, take more than five percent of an individual's time. In Chapter 8 Operations the difference between "work instructions" which are a series of tasks that apply to a process or procedure and "job descriptions" which include more generic tasks that apply to people are discussed. Chapter 10 Human Resources focuses more on job descriptions in general and performance reviews.

Each individual should have brought to the planning meeting copies of what they believe to be the purpose of their job and their 4-6 major responsibilities, and an estimate of the percent of time they spend annually on each to share with the leadership team. In this discussion it is important to start with the top leader in the organization. In general, it is the purpose of the top leader in the organization, whether there are three employees or three thousand, to:

"Coordinate all the resources of the organization to achieve the vision."

This can be worded many ways, and should be, to reflect the values and culture of the organization; but the basic purpose remains the same. However, the top leader's major responsibilities can vary greatly. You will remember that the top leader is always responsible for the *planning system* of the organization, thus the one responsibility that is consistent with all top leaders is:

"To facilitate, coordinate, coach and develop the current and future leaders of the organization in achieving the annual plan"

The amount of time spent doing this varies depending on the size of the organization. In a three-person organization this is probably 5-10 percent of the top leader's time. In a one hundred-person organization this responsibility probably takes half or more of the top leader's time.

It is important to note that "responsibility" implies a complete sentence with action verb(s). It is very common, but incorrect, for responsibilities to be listed as "finance" or "operations" or "marketing." But it is hard to hold someone accountable to those things if they never actually said exactly what they were going to do. Thus, complete, clear, concise sentences are important.

Often the top leader in a small organization has responsibility for one or more of the other major systems of the organization. Thus here are example purpose statements for each of the other major systems of the organizations, which become major responsibilities for the important people in small organizations:

<u>Marketing</u>: *To identify, attract, and retain customers that match the abilities and needs of the organization.*

<u>Operations</u>: *To ensure the on-time, on-quality, on-price[25] delivery of product and services of the organization.*

<u>Finance</u>: *To ensure accurate, timely and complete development, analysis and reporting of organizational financial information.*

<u>Human Resources</u>: *To ensure the availability, development, and retention of qualified individuals to meet the short and long-term goals of the organization.*

It is important to point out the difference between sharing tasks, and sharing responsibility. For example, the top leader in a small organization may share specific tasks (e.g. payroll or accounts payable) with a bookkeeper or similar position, but the responsibility for ensuring timeliness, accuracy, completeness etc. remain with the top leader position. Alternately, in a larger organization there may be a specific person whose <u>purpose</u> is as described in the above Finance example, and who has specific responsibilities related to payroll, accounts payable, and accounts receivable (as examples) and has staff to perform related tasks.

Managing each major system (planning, marketing, operations, finance & HR) of the organization is ALWAYS either the purpose of someone's position, or someone's responsibility!

In completing the listing of all major responsibilities for the top leader, keep in mind that no person should have more than seven major responsibilities – especially the top leader. As previously indicated, percentages of time should be estimated for each responsibility. Do not worry too much about the estimated times if this is the first time you have tried to do this. I usually recommend that at some point in the future the leaders do an actual time study to get a closer measure of the actual proportion of time spent on the various responsibilities. The purpose of the time estimates is to help individuals understand their own, and others' priorities.

Since these responsibilities are still just possibilities (that is no one has committed to them yet), the next step is to define COS for each responsibility. Just as with the possibilities step, some responsibilities may have only one condition of satisfaction; others may have several. Again there should be no more than seven COS for any one responsibility, with fewer, clearer better. One simple condition of satisfaction for a marketing position might be:

The organization achieves at least X in sales for the period (year?).

Remember these are COS and should not be dreams. The person involved will be held accountable to achieving these, so both parties (team and individual) need to agree up front that each condition of satisfaction is reasonable and possible. It can also be agreed that a given COS is a stretch goal, but in that case a minimum goal should be defined in addition. Also, it is valuable to have both subjective and objective COS (and an equal amount of each) to ensure that a wide range of outcomes are considered.

Once the listing of purpose, major responsibilities, time estimates, and COS for the top leader are completed, everyone (including the top leader) should answer the question:

"If Beatrice achieves the COS for her respective responsibilities, would everyone agree that she is doing her job?"

Assuming everyone says yes then you move on to the next person and have people add their tasks to meet each condition of satisfaction. Often people already have a list of tasks, and they just need to apply them to the appropriate COS. If someone says no to the question posed above, that means that a condition of satisfaction is missing. To address this the nay respondent is asked to clarify what would need added to make him or her comfortable.

In moving on to the next person, the same sequence is used as identified in the Planning Pyramid. That is, next in line is the person responsible for Marketing, then Operations, then Finance, and finally Human Resources. In small companies the roles may be shared such that this sequence is not perfectly possible. The process should simply be done as accurately as possible, remembering that refinement can come later. In each case you want everyone to agree to the final conditional question.

Once Clear Responsibilities for each leader present are established, *responsibilities can be assigned for the action items for each COS associated with each strategy in the strategic plan.* This is the basis of the <u>Annual Business Plan</u>. At this point most of the action items should be obvious. However, in some cases you may find time conflicts that have to be addressed. For example, the addition of a major piece of equipment could be a challenge for an already beleaguered operations person. If this is the case a decision must be made as to whether he/she can hand off tasks or responsibilities to others (either those on the team or others who are part of the operations group), to free up time to implement this major project. Alternately it might be decided to outsource certain activities. This is another example of why responsibility for action items is not assigned until now. In view of the fact that there may be things that are important for the organization to accomplish that might be outsourced to someone with the skills and abilities to do well (in many cases better than if done internally) it is worth considering outsourcing before moving to finalize assignment of responsibilities. The decision to outsource creates an additional action item.

In developing the responsibilities list it may also become apparent that there is a group of very important tasks that no one has the time or experience to do presently. A common example is that the growth of the organization has increased the number of HR related tasks such that a full or half time HR person is needed to implement them. Thus hiring such a person, or redefining responsibilities of an existing employee may be necessary. Such an eventuality may have been foreseen earlier in the process (in the assessment phase). But if not, it is here that hiring an HR person becomes a new *strategy*, with COS, related action items and responsibilities.

The next step in the process is to identify how success will be measured and celebrated. This is referred to as the Recognition stage.

Recognition

The purpose of the final stage of the planning process is to clearly define how you will know: are your actions proceeding positively (according to or similar to plan), when are critical  intermediate steps occurring, how you will hold each other accountable, how you will decide when to adjust activities, and when you will celebrate successes.

Often called the benchmarking process, this recognition stage is a critical part of project implementation. The simplest, most common, and most straightforward way to evaluate progress on a plan is for the leadership team to meet monthly, when monthly financial reports are available, and to review specific progress toward the plan based on benchmarks set during the planning process.

Here each major strategy and the timeline of identified actions are examined against progress to date. Additional intermediate steps and benchmarks may be identified at this point. An example of an intermediate step could be that in meeting the installation of the new piece of equipment by April 30th, it will need to be ordered by February 1st and on site by April 1st. Thus these become intermediate dates to measure and hold the process accountable to.

The old saying, if it's measured it's managed, holds true here. When people know that assigned responsibilities and deadlines will be discussed and that they will be held accountable they are much more likely to meet goals. In the same vein, things that are celebrated become habits. So celebrating accomplishments publically (e.g. with the whole staff either by posting or group meeting) reinforces positive behavior. Also celebrations are important for achieving closure on projects. Do not celebrate for "almost" being done. Celebrate completion. It is like a graduation ceremony that marks a time in an organization's history. You also want to be sure to appreciate attempts that don't work out as you expected or even fail. You want to encourage a proactive environment and judicious risk-taking; so showing appreciation for effort in the attempt is equally important.

Don't forget to plan for fun! Company barbecues, recognition of monthly birthdays and promotions with cakes, pizza parties for highly productive weeks or months - are all examples of ways to celebrate.

This whole process is about spreading responsibility, ensuring accountability and recognizing and acknowledging success. Including aspects of your organization that reflect your culture is critical. For example, the degree to which you are including social and environmental responsibility in your planning process, these things should be celebrated as well. People long to be part of something positive and constructive

85

in their lives. Making your organization a leader in that regard brings value to people's positions beyond money and builds the kind of community people want to be a part of.

To this point, development of a *Strategic Plan* and an *Annual Business Plan* has been discussed. A more detailed discussion of the four major systems is presented in the next few chapters to aid in defining and implementing improvement processes.

To the extent there are multiple people on the operations team, marketing team, and finance team (as denoted in the Organizational structure) separate plans are needed for each of those systems. Remember a plan is both about committing and communicating, and if multiple people are part of a system plans ARE NEEDED for that system. If only one person is involved or a system is simply one responsibility of a person, then a formal written plan would be valuable, but not necessary, as it should be effectively addressed in the job description.

The **Strategic Plan** include:
- Strategies
- COS for each strategy

Annual Business Plan include above PLUS:
- Person responsible for each COS
- Actions and dates for each COS
- Benchmarks for each Action

Looking Ahead

As suggested previously, the degree of detail an organization must go into in their plan depends on a number of different factors. In the next five chapters the four core systems of the organizations are discussed in some detail, to aid you in determining what might be missing in your organization that might help you become more successful, and to guide you in putting those pieces in place. Chapter 8 provides a primer on marketing, as it is the key strategic system in most organizations. Chapter 9 defines several approaches to finding new customers and growing the business profitably. Chapter 10 presents some fundamental ways to organize people to provide whatever goods or services the marketing activities have promised, whether these are the programs of a nonprofit, the services of an architect firm, or the products of a modern factory.

Chapter 11 presents a fairly unique look at financial reporting. Although the approach described herein looks deceptively simple, and probably close to what you are already doing, the devil is truly in the details. Small discrepancies in your measuring system can lead to big errors in decision-making. Many leaders have been shocked at how a simple change in how you do your financial reporting can dramatically change the way you view your business and ultimately financial success.

Chapter 12 discusses the basics approach to creating a culture of personal responsibility and accountability. Written job descriptions with clear and agreed on responsibilities, along with conflict resolution processes that lead to open, direct, positive communication can lead to regular performance reviews that result in continuous individual and ultimately organizational improvement.

Finally, lucky Chapter 13 assumes you have gleaned needed information from the previous chapters to put together a written plan of some sort, whether it is one page or a hundred, and focuses briefly on the implementation process. Plans aren't reports you write and forget them. They are a map through uncharted territory, the future, and a way to get you to your ultimate destination...prosperity.

Chapter 8
Marketing Systems26 101: 3-Ms, 4-Ps, and 5 Ss

Remember that best selling book "All I really need to know I learned in kindergarten" by Robert Fulgham?[27] In it he suggests that it is the little things in life - like playing fair, sharing, and cleaning up your own mess - that truly define who you are, your happiness, and your success. For many

organizations, the principles we learn in introductory marketing classes play that same role. It is the basic concepts of who is my customer, what do they want and need, and how can I make them happy that should drive the organization.

Marketing is among the most misunderstood of business activities. Often, the term marketing is used synonymously with sales. It is true that "sales" is one of the functions that occur within the overall marketing system; yet sales is simply one small component of a much broader marketing role that properly includes functions ranging from product conception and design to packaging, pricing, and service following the sale.

Given the broad role of marketing it is perhaps not surprising that for some products, marketing accounts for a majority of the product cost. To illustrate consider the twenty-cent product in the two-dollar package (e.g. a package with one bolt for two dollars versus a box of 50 bolts for ten dollars). Rationally, we might suggest that it is crazy to spend two-plus dollars for a twenty-cent part. Yet, the customer may well be achieving benefits from this approach beyond the specific needs addressed by the part (e.g. they don't have to buy 49 bolts they don't need – so from their point of view they save eight dollars!). It is the job of marketing to identify and assess such wants and needs, and to ensure that the organization's product offerings satisfy them.

Good marketing is the process by which organizations better understand the inner nature of those they wish to serve. Does the person looking for a pet cat have a problem with mice – or loneliness? Are they buying coffee for the flavor, the warmth, or the experience at the coffee shop? Is the person buying a boat seeking a means of transportation across water, or seeking a state-of-the art fishing craft, or are they buying quality time with their family? Not that many years ago one boat did it all. Today, astute marketers have identified the many independent customer needs and desires in boating and, as a result, there is a boat tailored for almost every use.

Background

Marketing can be defined as "those human activities directed at satisfying wants and needs through voluntary exchange processes." The most important takeaway from this Chapter is that there is a *critical sequence of events that needs to occur for a successful marketing outcome* i.e. one that satisfies the wants and/or needs of the customer and results in growth in revenues or profits for the organization. Activities that occur "out-of-sequence" are the cause of unnecessary or excessive expenditure of resources and often lead to an all-too-common focus by the customer on price as the only product attribute of merit. Here some simple guidelines—the 3-Ms, 4-Ps, and 5-Ss of marketing—are suggested as a means of optimizing your resources and maximizing the effectiveness of your marketing activities.

Alphabet Soup – the 3-Ms, 4-Ps, and 5-Ss of Marketing

Although not perfect in every situation, the following sequence is appropriate for a vast majority of markets, products, and situations. As a simple mnemonic these are described as the 3-Ms, 4-Ps and 5-Ss of Marketing. In general, an organized marketing process is crucial to gaining the right sales (profitable ones) from the right customers (e.g. ones that pay) at the right time (e.g. when they need it). The overall approach to the marketing process is to define the **M**arket you are trying to sell to, the Marketing **M**ix you are going to use to attract those customers, and the **M**essage you are going to use to get customers to adopt your product. *These are the 3-Ms of our marketing process.*

Markets

The first M - <u>Markets</u>, is defined as groups of people with the willingness and ability to buy your product that have definable distinguishing purchasing characteristics. In most instances "everyone" is not a market for your product. The biggest challenge for many companies is the process of defining exactly what customer they are actually after. For many this feels limiting and risky. *It is important to recognize that you are not restricting whom you will do business with, but rather carefully selecting those you are going to invest money in going after.* Given limited resources, you want to go after the kind of customer you are most likely to be successful with; that is one that you can serve really well, appreciates what you do, and is a match for your products, services, and values.

The market could be as big as everyone in the United States; although numerically and geographically quite large, seeking to appeal to this market would allow you to do your promotion in English. Moreover, Americans have a number of very definable characteristics. Alternately, you could refine your market further and target everyone within five hundred miles (a VERY common starting point) or define all businesses of a certain kind within five hundred miles as your core market. Alternatively, you might define your market by many other measures, e.g. all hunters in the United States. The secret to maximizing chances of success is to define the market clearly.

The next step is to divide the market into homogeneous segments, or customers that have very similar characteristics. A "good" market segment is based on a number of characteristics that are common to those within a given segment; those within a defined segment should be:

- Accessible (both for communication and supply),
- Sufficiently significant in terms of their current or potential purchasing requirements ability to meet the volume and financial needs of your organization (including profit potential),
- Clearly definable in terms of "uniqueness," and
- Likely to respond similarly to your marketing stimuli.

There are two subjective and two objective approaches to segmentation. The two most common objective approaches are segmenting by geographic location and demographic characteristics. The segmentation of the market based on lifestyle characteristics (sometimes referred to as psychographic segmentation) and behavior are more subjective approaches. Naturally, in large enough markets these approaches may be layered, such that you might focus on a segment that includes, for example, companies within 500 miles of your factory (geographic), that have male purchasing agents over the age of 35 (demographic) who like to fish (psychographic), and that tend to buy their products monthly in bulk (behavior). This might be a very good segment for your firm – if enough customers exist that meet these criteria and your financial goals.

Another example might be that, if the market you are after is all fishermen in the United States then three unique segments might include people that enjoy fly fishing, bass fishing, or deep sea fishing. Although all enjoy certain similarities and have some product purchases in common, separate marketing approaches to the three groups might be needed depending on exactly what you are trying to sell and how closely you need to align your organization with that segment.

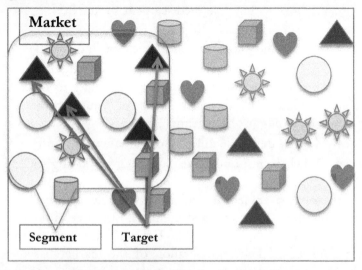

Finally you prioritize your market segments and pick <u>targets</u>. In the above example, if the goal is to sell pickup trucks that have a heavy duty towing package, bass fishermen might be identified as better targets than either fly fishermen (who don't necessarily use boats) or deep sea fishermen (whose boats may be too big to haul around). Fishermen in general may still be a good overall market for pickups, and all three segments offer realistic opportunities (and orders from any of them are not turned down), but bass fishermen might be the highest priority target segment. With regard to targeting, it is important that there be a clear and definable prioritization of the types of benefits valued by each target segment.

Marketing Mix

Once the target segment(s) have been selected, to the next task is to define the second of the 3 Ms, the Marketing Mix, or simply "Mix." *Each target segment may require its own unique marketing mix, or at the very least unique variations, to be successful!* The Marketing Mix is marketing language or jargon for the set of core programs that marketers use to define the tools used to attract and retain customers. *Here the second, and more common memory tool, the 4-Ps are used to describe these four tools.* The **four P's** are:

- **P**lace – the marketing channel, which includes those individuals or organizations between you and the end user (e.g. manufacturer's representative, distributor or retailer)
- **P**roduct – the bundle of perceived benefits the customer pays you for
- **P**rice – the strategy you use to gain the greatest combination of volume and value
- **P**romotion – the methods and tools you use to get your information in front of the customer in a manner that gets them to buy the product

Place

It is valuable to think of these as a sequence as well. That is, once a target audience is identified, you want to define the channel or **Place** through which you will reach your end customer. Each channel member will likely have additional and often independent benefits they seek from your product. Common differences are packaging and credit terms.

Product

After clearly defining the channel the benefits that can be provided with your **Product** to meet both the channel member's and target's specific needs can be refined. Customers value products as "bundles of benefits." The benefits perceived by the customer can be economic, social, or psychological. Services also fit in this description of products. Products have both tangible and intangible attributes. The difference between an attribute and a benefit is: an *attribute* is a characteristic of your product offering, while a *benefit* is the perceived value of that attribute to the customer. For example, an attribute of a certain car may be that it goes from 0-60 in 4.5 seconds. However, this may or may not be a benefit to a particular customer. To successfully design and sell products, it is important to recognize the difference between attributes and benefits! Ideally, those involved in product conception and design should know the perception of benefit by potential customers long before a new product is brought to the marketplace.

People value individual attributes differently. It is important to understand not only exactly what people are interested in, but also either how much they are interested or how important that attribute is to them. In a study a number of years ago of attributes offered by a hotel chain, one of the new "benefits" management felt they were providing and putting in every advertisement was the fact they offered fax service for the first time. The study did what was called an importance-performance analysis of a number of attributes about the hotel. In this type of study the researcher asks two questions about each attribute the hotel offers; basically, how well does the hotel provide this service, and how much do you care. What they found was that customers reported the hotel did a great job of providing a fax service, but nobody really cared. What they really did care about was a hot shower, a comfortable bed, and a clean room – and the hotel only did a mediocre job of providing those things. (Interestingly, one of the comments was, "instead of posting notices about the new fax machine, post the number of who to call when the hot water runs out!" Not a bad idea!)

Marketers also talk about *product extensions*, such as Nike's extension from shoes into other sportswear. Often most or even all the profits are in the product extensions, rather than in the generic product itself.

Augmentation is the process of allowing the customer to modify or add to a product in some way, such as the ability to customize athletic footwear to include team name and player number. Heated seats, sunroofs, and stereos are examples of how cars can be augmented.

Price

Once the full extent of the product to be sold has been clearly defined it is then possible to develop a **Price** strategy. An organization's pricing strategy is often the most neglected component of the marketing mix. Common strategies include:

- Penetration – a low price approach designed to grow market share (volume)
- Premium – a high price strategy based on unique features such as copyrights, patents, or innovation
- Competitive Bid – an approach based on the assumption that there are a number of suppliers relatively equally capable of providing the benefits the customer seeks

Many companies assume that a "competitive bid" approach means that the customer treats all benefits equally and that the bottom line cost is all that matters. Indeed many quoting processes start that way. But in reality this is rarely true.

Each individual purchaser and each individual organization has a priority list of benefits of which price is generally a top 4 item, but is rarely the number one item. It is vital to understand a customer's priority list and to price the attributes of products separately based on the priority of the benefits perceived by the customer.

With a bit of thinking it is possible to identify product attributes that are highly competitive, but also some that are much harder to create while at the same time valued by customers. For example, suppose a customer requests a cabinet that is environmentally friendly, and that specific "green materials" (e.g. recycled barn timbers for cabinet frame and doors) for that cabinet costs the organization an additional 15%. For the past twenty years it has been common for makers of products like this to raise the total price of this greener version AT LEAST 15% (often 25% or even 50%) more than for the traditional version, with the common result that the customer decides the green one is too expensive and buys the original version (and the manufacturer is relieved).

This is an example of a complete failure of an organization's pricing model and a missed opportunity to take advantage of a customer's clear declaration of a high priority benefit that the supplier is not fulfilling. The outcome of this mistake is a less satisfied customer than otherwise might occur and a significant missed opportunity to make more money on the sale!

To illustrate a better approach to pricing, in the case of the cabinet above, we can estimate the cost of the materials the customer want replaced with green versions represent a third the actual selling price of the final product. Thus, an increase of 15% in the cost for these green materials actually reflects an increase in the final product of just under 5% (15% times 33%). *Thus any price you can get above 5% more for the "greener" version is gravy.* So, if the green cabinet were offered for 7-8% more, providing exactly what the customer wants for a minimal up charge, this would reflect an increase in net profitability of almost 50% (assuming the company has an average net profit of 6% annually). Of course, if average net profit is less than 6% this has an even bigger affect!!

Let's look at a more-detailed comparison for clarification:

	Product #1	Green Version
Doors & Frame Cost	$99 (33%)	$114 (up 15%)
Labor & other Materials	$120 (40%)	$120 (same)
Overhead	$66 (22%)	$66 (same)
Total Cost	$285	$300 (up 5%)
Selling Price	$300	$324 (up 8%)
Profit	$15 (5%)	$24 (up 60%!!)

Companies that have been assuming they need to charge *at least* the % additional cost of the wood for the total product, and not getting the business (or not getting it as a green version) have been missing a HUGE opportunity to have a significant effect on their bottom line. This example is also true for ALL BENEFITS that the customer ranks as a very high priority, green or otherwise. Good pricing programs value individual benefits carefully and recognize that there are certain attributes of a product that are very competitive, and some that are not. Distinguishing between them and pricing accordingly is critical to maximizing profitability.

Promotion
The fourth **P** is **Promotion,** and is the activity most commonly thought of as the exclusive realm of marketing. The dominant components of promotion are Advertising and Publicity. Generally, advertising is something you pay for and publicity is something you get for free. In practice, companies may spend a large amount of money getting "free"

publicity, but those costs are generally internal using existing resources such as people's time and talent.

Advertising today can be broken into at least the following categories:

- Print information (E.g. newspapers, magazines, brochures, Flyers, etc.)
- Electronic Media (Radio, TV, Smart phone, Internet, etc.)
- Human (Personal selling)

Publicity is generated by activities such as sponsoring events such as little league teams, races, and charities or by contributing articles to newspapers and magazines.

Once the target segment is known, the channel to be used in reaching the target market defined, a clear definition of product benefits identified, and a pricing strategy decided, advertising is defined by the message to be conveyed to potential customers.

Message
The purpose of an organization's promotional activities is to get the organization's **Message** (3rd M) to the Target segment. For many organizations, communication with the intent of convincing people to engage in some desired behavior is a critical function. Whether seeking to convince someone to buy a product or service, support a position on a political issue, or change personal behavior (e.g., smoking) - communication requires framing messages such that recipients can understand them and are motivated to respond accordingly. While the most critical component of what many organizations do, all too often very little thoughtful planning is put into the messaging process.

Messaging

The goal of a messaging process is to inspire the greatest possible number of people to adopt a product, service or idea. It is the role of the "marketing message" to lead targeted individuals through the sequential "product" adoption process – where in this case the word "message" refers to an actual product, any service, or an idea. In addition, "audience" and "target market" are used interchangeably to denote the applicability of this process in both selling something and influencing opinions.

The 5-Step Message Adoption Process

1. *Awareness*
2. *Interest*
3. *Evaluation*
4. *Trial*
5. *Adoption*

The *message adoption process* has five sequential stages: *Awareness, Interest, Evaluation, Trial, and Adoption.* It is critical to recognize the importance of this sequence, and the variability in the components of the message required at each stage.

1. Awareness Stage

Getting people aware of your message is more complex than having them simply recognize the name of your product, the brand, or the logo – although all those things may help with the awareness building campaign. The *Awareness* stage is successful when the target audience is able to envision your message as a realistic possibility for themselves. This is often the hardest stage to get past, and can be the most difficult to interpret based only on the initial response of the target market. Those comprising the target market or audience may ask general questions during the awareness stage to get a basic understanding of what the message is, implying but not confirming interest. Sometimes the ONLY way to know if an audience views a message as applicable to them is by asking them directly (e.g., would you vote for so and so?).

Target market sampling can be used with groups to estimate the effectiveness of the message in getting past this stage (e.g., asking a random sample of individuals from the group).

As mentioned above, in many ways the Awareness stage can be the *most difficult stage to get through.* This results from the fact that consumers (i.e., you, me and the rest of the human population!) have a toolset of behaviors that protect them from unwanted inputs. It is fairly well accepted that these defensive behaviors are learned, and although they may vary greatly from culture to culture there are some commonalities.

Pavlov[28] described the behavioral sequence such as that needed to get past these defensive filters as the "stimulus response" method, by which there is a) a *cue* or weak stimulus that directs the attention (e.g., smell), b) a *drive* or motivation that reflects the need (e.g., hunger), c) a *response* to eliminate that need (e.g., buy some cookies), and d) *reinforcement* of the action, either positive or negative (e.g., positive, the cookies taste good – or negative, your mom yells at you for eating cookies before dinner).

To apply this theory to the messaging process, marketers have adopted what is commonly referred to as the "Black Box[29]" Model of human behavior (where the Black Box is the mind). So, in order to create true product Awareness the message must generate a <u>cue</u> that carries the information past a series of filters in the target audience's mind including selective:

- Exposure (precursor to cue – e.g., what radio or TV stations we choose or person to person sales)
- Attention (does the cue attract the senses? – sight, smell, taste, etc.)
- Comprehension (how we interpret the cue/message)
- Retention (do we remember it and how important it is? – high emotion leads to high retention!)

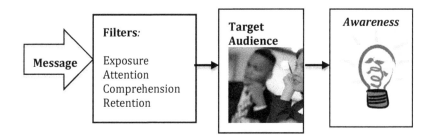

These filters serve to protect against information overload. In addition, every individual brings a different experience, a different set of evaluation criteria, and different attitudes to the problem recognition (or drive) process. Thus individual personalities greatly affect responses to different messages.

<u>Use of Data to get Through Filters</u>
Too often companies use data (pricing etc.) too early in the marketing process in an attempt to differentiate themselves. A marketing message is unlikely to forge a way through emotionally charged filters by use of data. Data is primarily applicable in the *Evaluation* stage and may in fact be highly negative for many individuals during the Awareness stage of the message adoption process. Since communication stages are sequential, a message shouldn't try to convince an audience of a product's statistical benefits until the process has progressed through individual filters and triggered Interest. This is a critically important point. When customers are not making "rational decisions" based on convincing data it may be because an organization hasn't done a good job of (or has

> Data is primarily applicable in the *Evaluation* stage and may in fact be highly negative for many individuals at the *Awareness* stage of the process.

completely skipped) leading individuals through the first two stages of the message adoption process.

The use of appropriate messages targeted at triggering the interests, or <u>drives</u>, of specific market segments is often the only way to get to the point where an audience can be induced to evaluate details that may lead to the desired <u>response</u>, or to a trial. Positive <u>reinforcement</u> follows. Underlying this approach is an assumption that the different wants and needs of the target market have been researched and fully understood.

Crafting Messages to Get Past Filters

A target audience is defined by segmenting the overall market into target groups based on common demographic, geographic, psychographic and/or behavioral characteristics. For messaging purposes the focus should be more on the psychographic (activities, interests, and opinions) and behavioral (perceived benefit) characteristics to define a target audience.

The first step in crafting messages is to develop an intimate understanding of the target market's wants and needs – basically creating the knowledge of what <u>drives</u> those in the target group so appropriate <u>cues</u> can be developed to trigger the desired <u>response</u> and create behaviors that can then be <u>reinforced</u>.

The next step is to craft a *unique message campaign for each unique target market* (audience segment). The first objective is to identify the best path to get past filters; one approach is to begin by addressing the following:

- Selective *exposure* – Basically answering the question of "how to get in front of the target market?" It is important to understand characteristics such as which TV stations/shows those comprising the target market watch (beer drinkers watch football), which radio stations they listen to (organic foods customers tend to listen to NPR), or which magazines they read (maybe trade magazines?) in order to select the right venue or channel for a messaging campaign. The wood products industry, for example, is known for personal selling – similar to the very successful girl-scout cookie model.

- Selective *attention* - It is essential to understand the right cues (beer drinking men might pay attention to girls in bikinis; environmentalists might react to images of
environmental devastation). There are three basic ways to get peoples' attention – aural (hear it – e.g. radio), visual (see it – e.g. show them samples) and physical (do it – e.g. test drive[30]) and all three are valid methodologies and can complement one another. Today, through a vehicle such as YouTube, organizations have the ability for the first time in history to provide "hear and see" information simultaneously to a potentially vast audience at low cost. This can be a great way also to address the physical, as activities can be demonstrated in detail to simulate experience.

- Selective *comprehension* – Here the challenge is to ensure that the message is in a form that people can readily understand …not too complicated, not too simple. However, better too simple than too complicated. Simple language accompanied by straightforward images is generally best. Remember the old saying, "a picture is worth a thousand words?" Good advice, but the picture selected is extremely important. In seeking to achieve comprehension it is particularly important to remember the importance of addressing behavioral characteristics; in other words, it is here where it is important to portray benefits. In this regard, an emphasis on outcomes is vastly better than focusing on the details of achieving them. Thus hospitals don't show images of bloody open-heart surgery to promote their services, but rather happy retired couples playing with their grandchildren. Wood products companies don't show pictures of people cutting down trees, but rather beautiful furniture or cozy homes. The goal here is for the target audience to begin to perceive the benefits of whatever product or message is being promoted: health, a sustainable environment, product quality, or world peace.

- Selective *retention* – The goal at this stage is that messages make an impact on the target's memory systems. Emotions are especially important in causing people to remember things. Humor is commonly used as it engages positive emotions that are fairly straightforward to create. Fear is another easily created emotion, but not one recommended for use in most instances, although it is among the most common used in some venues (e.g., politics). Other positive emotions come from creating situations where the targets can either see themselves or other people (and particularly influential people) enjoying the benefits of adopting whatever is being promoted. This latter characteristic is a very important one as it denotes the importance of *reference groups* to influencing people's decisions.

The Role of Reference Groups

Reference groups can be an important part of the messaging process, as they can be the largest influence on an individual's attitudes, opinions, values, and behavior. Reference groups affect the way you remember information - that is, what emotional reaction you associate with that memory. Types of reference groups include: Associative (people you view positively), Disassociative (people you view negatively), and Aspirational (people you would like to emulate).

Creating an associative memory can be accomplished by showing the target audience people they perceive as similar to themselves enjoying the benefits of the product adoption or behavior you want to encourage (perhaps a mom racing through the winding hills in her new minivan). An example of a message intended to create a disassociative memory might be showing a villain driving a competitor's car on those same roads…. crashing. Organizations use movie stars to create aspirational association with their products (e.g., for some people, if Derek Jeter uses it… it must be good).

Importance of The Messenger

Based on people's reaction to the last example (Tiger Woods) it is possible to understand the importance of attuning the messenger to the needs of the target audience. For some people a professional golfer will be a trusted and admired source of behavior stimulus (perhaps an aspirational reference), while for others, he may be quite the opposite. It is important that the messenger match the audience, the more complex and/or emotional the topic, the more important the messenger.

The use of testimonials is one way to supplement the message and balance any potential negative impacts of a specific messenger. Short testimonials from a variety of individuals (with different

> *The more complex the message and/or emotional behavior you are trying to influence, the more important the messenger!*

marketing profiles) can be used to aid getting through the target's filters and help the individual identify with the desired behaviors. Example (fake) testimonials could include:

- *"With Super Multigrain toaster waffles my kids now get a nutritional breakfast they enjoy."* – Joan, mother of 4 in Houston
- *"The QZ9 truck provides the power I need in any weather and great dependability."* – Joe, professional truck driver
- *"I've used this drug for years and it's never let me down."* – Dr. Arnold Wolfowitz, cardiac surgeon

Testimonials can be highly effective and are fairly easily implemented. In some situations these are referred to as second party certification. There are also third party certifications (e.g., organic or forest certification) that can aid in the sale of some products to some target markets.

Finally, for certain kinds of behaviors, where significant distrust or emotional links exist, the messenger may become more critical than the message. For complex messages such as environmental ones the credentials of the messenger and the venue through which a person receives the message are critical. For example, a poster in a video game store with a testimonial by Carrot Top[31] may not be the best place to get the general public to believe in climate change – whereas a documentary hosted by Tom Brokaw on PBS might have a significant impact on those same people.

Although this has varied somewhat historically, people trust the opinions of (in approximately the following order):

1. Family & Friends
2. Consumer opinions posted online
3. Educational and Medical experts (e.g., PhDs and MDs)
4. Other experts specific to issue (e.g., electricians on electrical issues, plumbers on plumbing)
5. Industry
6. State and Federal Government [12, 25]

2. Interest Stage

Once you have successfully passed through someone's filters and gotten their attention enough to consider your information, the next step is to clarify attributes and benefits for that audience. This is likely to require a different message than is used to achieve someone's awareness. Depending on the nature of the attributes you are trying to explain, a different messenger may even be valuable! Here the primary goal of the process is to clarify the nature of the attributes and benefits that will appeal to your target audience. As above, selecting the right information to provide that is likely to attract their interest is critical to moving them through the adoption process.

The audience demonstrates their *Interest* by asking questions of clarification and detail about specific attributes of the message. For example they might ask, "Do you mean they actually replant trees? Or can this really translate fifty languages fluently?" Generally at the Interest stage the questions are much more specific and there are more of them than at the awareness stage. The point here is that the information at the interest stage must go into a higher level of detail, and this is only possible either through direct customer feedback (e.g., questions) or by extensive research into the wants and needs of the customer. You can tell if you have successfully gotten someone's interest if they start making comparisons! This leads you to…

3. Evaluation Stage

In the *Evaluation* stage the audience or target market is ready to make direct comparisons to alternatives. These comparisons may be obvious; such as they say: "I can buy it at Wal-Mart cheaper", or more indirect such as "you're too high." As all good sales people recognize, the exact language of the customer is critical and marketers are often the greatest sticklers for semantics around. For example, the phrase "you're too expensive" is likely to mean the comparison is to their available funds while the term "you're too high" implies your price is compared to a competitor's product of perceived equal value. Neither of these interpretations is 100% true all of the time, but is indicative of the kinds of interpretation necessary at the evaluation stage.

Every good sales person also knows that once a target begins making comparisons he or she is well down the path toward a legitimate adoption of your product or idea, assuming you have selected the right target in the first place. It is not suggested here that it is possible to convert Satan, merely that if the right audience is selected and presented with the right message delivered in the right manner; there is a legitimate probability of getting them to adopt your message. The goal of the Evaluation stage messaging process is to demonstrate the superiority of a product or idea. Again, videos, test-drives, all of those things that get people's attention can often be a component of the evaluation process, but subtle differences exist. Clarifying the benefits is critical at this stage whereas exploration of attributes can be successful at the earlier stages.

4. Trial Stage

The *Trial* stage is the easiest to identify as individuals actually undertake to implement the behavior that you are trying to encourage for the first time, e.g., they vote the way you want or begin to buy what you are selling. With ideas it is a bit more complicated. Generally, the trial phase with an idea means they begin exploring it with others, testing how the arguments hold up when they try to utilize them. Success of course brings further ingraining of the idea into someone's belief system.

The trial phase is the opportunity to ask the individual for the order, or in the case of the idea, to ask "what do you think?" This provides the opportunity for the individual to voice remaining concerns, unexplored needs for comparison, or areas of information that are lacking. In the sales world this is all part of what is often referred to as the "trial close", but is equally valuable in exploring ideas with each other.

In any case, *getting people to act differently than they have can be extremely difficult*, as changing people's existing behaviors is generally much more difficult than creating new ones. For example, if someone has already fully and happily adopted a competing product there is a lot of work involved in starting back at the beginning with a new one! As a result, the number of filters a person puts up to prohibit unwanted information is very high in these situations. Thus the level of trust required to get past these filters, get people's attention, and get them to act differently is very high. Recognizing this and putting the appropriate effort and planning into the whole messaging process is critical to having any influence in changing the way people believe or act.

5. Adoption Phase

The *Adoption* stage is simply a measure of repeatability. Have they adopted your message consistently – meaning are they regularly buying something (e.g., loyal customers) or voting consistently, or acting regularly in the manner you hoped? Getting the target through this stage requires post trial stage follow through, message reinforcement, and benefit clarification.

> *Behaviors become habits when positively reinforced*

One of the critical and often neglected aspects of the adoption phase is the "post purchase" reinforcement process. It is critical to recognize, acknowledge, and reward individuals for positive behaviors. This acknowledgement process over an extended period of time builds up the kinds of filters for your competition that you want and need.

Above all, it is vital to recognize that marketing communication is all about people. The more that is known about the target audience and the more effort put into understanding them, the greater the likelihood of success. Finally, follow up and reinforcement are important. Behaviors become habits when positively reinforced.

Delivering a message to the right people, in the right way, at the right time, and through the right venue maximizes the chances of success.

Bottom Line

There is a *critical sequence of events that needs to occur for a successful marketing* outcome that results in revenue growth. Activities that occur "out-of-sequence" are the cause of unnecessary or excessive expenditure of resources and often lead to an all-too-common focus by the customer on price as the only product attribute of merit. In this Chapter some simple guidelines have been suggested—the 3-Ms, 4-Ps, and 5-Ss of marketing—as a means to optimize your resources and maximize the effectiveness of your marketing activities.

Chapter 9
Finding New Markets32

Over the years it has been common to hear individuals use the terms "markets" and "products" interchangeably. Yet markets are groups of people while products are bundles of benefits, usually goods or services. Thus the process of finding new markets is solely about finding more or different people who might buy your product. From the previous Chapter you may remember that a market is defined as people with:

> ➤ Needs to satisfy,
> ➤ Money and ability to spend,
> ➤ Willingness to spend

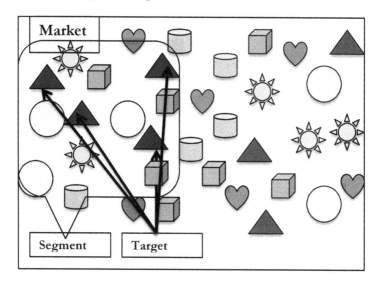

You may also recall that a good market was defined as one that is accessible, of sufficient size, unique in some way, and likely to respond to your marketing efforts. As a reminder, the image above demonstrates the market segmentation and targeting process.

What is the first step in finding new markets?

It comes as a surprise to many that there are a number of steps that must be taken internally <u>prior</u> to looking around externally for new customers. To begin, an organization should consider:

- What products do we make money on?
- What products would we make money on if we sold more of them?
- What products do we like to sell?
- Who is our favorite customer and why?
- What do we do well?
- What do our current customers think we do well, and which things are important to them?

Once these questions have been answered, a profile emerges of the kind of new customer you would like to have and the products and product features you might offer them. Once this is known, you can begin the process of deciding where to look!

What Products do we make money on?
This seems obvious once you think about it, but it is also really common for businesses to NOT know which products are their most or least profitable. This ignorance usually results from the fact that many firms evaluate profits in total, rather than by individual product groupings. Total profit margins can seriously decrease when an organization dominantly or even modestly expands in less profitable product lines. Without careful planning, organizations can accidentally "succeed" at selling more stuff they don't make

112

money on into new markets, and end up competing solely on price. Alternately, expanding the most profitable product lines can have significantly positive impacts on total profit margins. Even a small percentage of additional sales in very profitable products, has a huge impact on total profitability. Careful internal analysis is required to understand not only which products make the most money, but also *why* they are the most profitable. Are they profitable because they are the cheapest to produce, because customers are willing to pay more for them, or perhaps because your organization is uniquely qualified to make them?

What products would we make money on if we sold more of them?
A slight variation on the previous question brings into consideration the issue of volume. In general, companies completely understand the concept that an increase in volume of sales can cause efficiencies in operating and provide purchasing power with vendors. The caveat here is to recognize that volume based activities have what are called *optimum sales-operational points*. That is, if you plot the volume of sales versus expenses it is generally not a straight line but rather one with waves (ups and downs). In some cases, this volume/sales graph actually appears as a frequency or sine wave. This results from the fact that volume based sales increase in profitability as sales increase, dependent on a given set of expenses. At some point though, it becomes necessary to add a forklift, or more storage, or a service person. When these expenses are added the organization's net profitability often goes down at least temporarily. Thus it is really valuable to know where your firm currently is on the profitability curve for each product. An organization should also identify points where profits are optimized, where additional expenses are necessary, and, specifically where an increase in the volume of sales would really help the profits

of a particular product line (e.g. to better utilize some special equipment or personnel).

What products do we like to sell?
Companies are often surprised by this question. A common response is "what has our liking it got to do with it? It's the customer's opinion that matters!" The answer is that, sure, the customer's opinion absolutely rules. However, the combination of finding products that your customer really likes to buy and that the firm really likes to sell can be a winning combination. For example, perhaps all Porsche salespeople should be teenage boys. They have memorized every detail about the cars and have boundless enthusiasm for them – even when they may have never even driven one. This kind of enthusiasm could result in higher profitability. The idea is to harness the energy that comes with personal interest and apply it to your business. Cirrus, one of the most successful small private airplane manufacturers today, and Google are great examples of this approach. These firms specifically hire people that love, not just like, their respective product lines in the belief that those who feel passion for the products they sell would translate to enthusiastic customers and organizational growth.

When trying to figure out what products you like to sell it is very valuable to ask all levels of the organization. A top-selling product favored by executives may provide an ongoing headache for those on the production floor and a drain on creativity and energy. It is important to get broad input and to clearly understand discrepancies in views of various products and product lines.

Who is our favorite customer and why?
If your organization only asks staff one question about current practices, this is the most important one. It is critical to your success and growth that you understand and are able

to define the characteristics of the customer with whom you really enjoy doing business. *The response to this question tells you a tremendous amount about your own firm and the people in it.*

There are countless examples of companies that struggle with a customer or customers but fear addressing the issue, as they don't want to risk losing the sales volume. The customer just doesn't appear to appreciate what you do for some reason and there is always something wrong. Your price is too high, service too slow, quality is wrong or you never do the right thing. Basically, what you have is a poor values match; that is, this customer doesn't value the same things you do the same way. It is hard if not impossible to make money servicing a company with a poor values match.

When an organization clearly defines whom they like to do business with they get a better picture of both prospective customers and themselves. This self-awareness is critically important when trying to expand because this is the opportunity to take a core identity and create growth based on that. Lots of firms have grown organically over the years, basically taking whatever business came across their bow with little consideration of what they liked and disliked. It was dominantly about survival. But growth and finding new markets can be a different matter, and can positively affect the organization in ways well beyond increased revenues; and it may provide you with the opportunity to "fire" those customers that employees dislike.

It is important to be specific and comprehensive in evaluating what you like about the customer. Is it their buyer? Then why? Is it the fact they pay promptly? Do they buy stuff no one else seems to want, or do they pay extra to get exactly what they want? Is it the fact they buy weekly, or monthly, or give you an annual contract? It is important to identify exactly and completely everything you like about your favorite customer(s) and use that as your customer profile, or target, in the new market segment you expand into.

What do we believe we do well?
It is important to ask this question internally as well as of your customers. Internally the process is pretty straightforward. It is a very good idea to generate a list of your product's attributes and ask your employees to rank how well they think the organization does in providing them to customers. With employees it is very valuable to allow the opportunity to respond beyond a simple ranking. For example, you could ask for comments, or "any exceptions" about the particular attribute. That way an employee could rank something like on-time shipping with a five and add a comment like "except for Sandra's locksmith shop, whose orders we always seem to ship late for some reason." The more information you can get from employees in this process the better.

What do our customers think we do well and how important is it to them?
One of the best tools for evaluating this question is called the Importance-Performance Grid. This marketing tool not only evaluates what you do well but also provides insight into how much your customer cares. There are many examples of companies expending energy on things that they do well, but that their customer doesn't fully appreciate for one reason or another. Rather than trying to convince a customer they ought to care, a firm's energy is better spent in figuring out what they may already care more about.

A fairly simple way to do an importance-performance analysis is to give each of your customers a sheet of paper with the same list of organizational attributes on both sides. Attributes are things like guaranteed on time delivery, ninety-day credit terms, free shipping, fax machine available, and every part individually wrapped. It is ok to list up to twenty different attributes in a random order. Be sure to include all the ones you care about. Then, on one side of the paper you ask your customer to rank your performance on each attribute by putting a number from 1, poor performance, to 5, excellent performance, beside each attribute. Next, on the opposite side of the paper, you ask the customer to rank how important each attribute is to them, by putting a number from 1, unimportant, to 5, extremely important, beside each attribute.

You end up with a series of attributes for which you have information as to how well you perform and how much the customer cares for each. This is very valuable information for reviewing how well you are doing for an individual customer, and is valuable as well for identifying how the marketplace views your organization in general. For purposes of finding new markets, you care mostly about the latter and about the response of your "favorite" customer.

To evaluate this further, it is worthwhile to plot the answers on a graph that looks like the one to the left, with Performance results plotted 1 to 5 from left to right and Importance values plotted from bottom to top, and with the intersection representing a value of 3 for performance and 3 for importance. As an example, if the attribute "free shipping" received a 5 for performance and a 2 for importance you'd plot a point that was 5 to the right (all the way) and 2 up from the bottom (or halfway between the very bottom and the intersection, or about where the star is.

Those attributes that fall into Quadrant II are the ones you should promote in new markets.

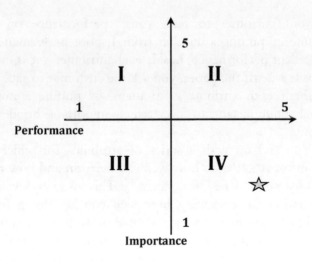

You can then plot the attributes for each customer, or average the responses of all customers for each attribute. Attributes that show up in quadrant I represent a problem: these are things that are important to customers but that your organization doesn't do well.

Attributes in this quadrant require immediate attention and investment. You need improvement quickly. If an attribute falls into quadrant II this means that the customers generally feel you do it well, and it is important to them that you do that. Keep up the good work and keep improving on the attributes in this quadrant. If the attributes ranking lands it in quadrant III, it means that you don't do this very well but customers in general don't care. So don't put much effort here. That doesn't mean that you should completely ignore these factors; it just means this is not a place to put your resources. Finally, if an attribute's ranking falls in quadrant IV, it means that you do a very good job at providing these attributes, but they aren't really important to your customers. Sometimes this means you should de-emphasis some of these attributes, particularly if they are places you have invested significant resources. Alternatively, an appropriate strategy is to simply not worry about these attributes and to not invest much time into maintaining them.

In summary, all the attributes that are in the top half of the grid are things you should put resources into. And for expansion purposes, those attributes that fall into quadrant II (which you do well and are important to the customers) are the ones you promote in new markets. These are the strengths that matter.

Internal Summary

Once you have done an internal analysis, you have a clear view of what defines the "ideal" customer –one you like to do business with and who buys products you make money on. You also know which products you want to grow in general, which ones would benefit from a little specific growth attention, your organization's strengths and weaknesses, and those attributes that are both important to the marketplace and that you do very well. This is a lot of good information.

If you do not have an existing "ideal" customer, then you should define one. This definition should have all of the characteristics of market segmentation so that your sales force knows what they are looking for. And don't forget to include the attribute rankings in this process. For example, a description of your ideal customer might look like the example below. Finding a new customer is significantly easier if you know what you are looking for. Then it is just a matter of where to look.

Our ideal customer:
> *Is located within 500 miles of our facility (geographic),*
> *Is in a community of 50,000 that is growing at a rate of 5 percent or more (demographic), Has purchasing agents that like*

to fish *(psychographic)*, and who buy at least half truckload quantities per month of our product *(behavior)*,

➢ *Appreciates the attributes we emphasize (e.g. fast delivery and service),*
➢ *Buys products that are profitable for us,*
➢ *Pays our invoices promptly, and*
➢ *Respects our employees and our business.*

Next steps

To a certain extent, the definition of your ideal customer will help to define where you expand to next. If there are potential additional ideal customers in your existing territory, then that may be the best place to focus your efforts. And never negate a potential new customer just because they appear loyal to your competition. To a certain extent, your competitor's best and most loyal customer is your ideal target. Efforts need not have an objecting of getting all the business, but simply to gain a small share of what could later become significant business activity.

Segmentation

Segmentation is the process of dividing the overall market into manageable chunks. Most companies start by doing this geographically. However, there are often very good reasons for staying within an existing region. When an organization decides to expand within an existing geographical region it is called "increasing the market penetration." The most common rationale for marketing more intensively within an existing region is that this provides an opportunity to utilize existing infrastructure more fully or to at least limit the amount of additional infrastructure necessary to achieve market growth. In some cases the type of product being sold (e.g. snowshoes) may effectively limit the potential sales region.

There are a number of ways to increase market penetration, the most common of which is to simply hire more salespeople and send them out to sell stuff. However, it may be that the best thing you can do is to more effectively use the present sales force. For example, subdividing an existing sales territory into smaller segments sometimes makes sense. In this case most of the components of the marketing mix (promotional pieces, pricing methods, and delivery methods) effectively stay about the same. Subdividing territories is fairly simple, allows the manager to use existing sales pros to manage the new sub-territories, and the segmentation process can also keep top sales staff "motivated." My brother-in-law was the top sales person in a large electrical firm. Over a thirty-year period his territory was regularly segmented (i.e. reduced) until, over time it went from being all of New England to just four or five select accounts. During all that change he remained the top sales person in the organization as he kept focusing his highly skilled efforts on a narrower and narrower region or customer base. This is an example of achieving market penetration by stimulating the competitive nature of skilled sales staff.

An alternate method of increasing market penetration is to divide an existing market by some other means, such as demographic, psychographic, or behavior characteristics. As one option, an organization might have sales people that specialize in certain size accounts throughout the region (e.g. very large or very small ones) because of some common unique behaviors within that group (e.g. they buy full truckloads of your product). Alternately you might have sales people that specialize in certain product applications, e.g. industrial versus retail. And it is very common to have overlap in these approaches, i.e. the market is divided into territories, but specialists call on certain types of clients across territories to aid the territory representative.

Finally, it is important to think outside the box when trying to identify new markets within a geographic region. It is, for example, important to be open to customers that require the same organizational attributes regardless of which of the traditional segment they fall into, e.g. a commercial construction client may be more similar to an industrial business than to a residential construction client.

It is often a good idea to first look at increasing market penetration before expanding geographically.

If geographical expansion is determined to be the best option for market growth, the next question is where and how. Often, a growing organization simply identifies a likely neighboring region with similar characteristics, duplicates their marketing programs from the initial region and voila they've expanded. To a certain extent it is that simple. But it is important to recognize the actual skills are that you are applying to the existing region and to recognize that straying beyond those skills can be difficult.

Finding your "position"
Traditionally, positioning of a product or organization is defined as "creating an image in the eye of the customer." This is one of the most important concepts in marketing, and all sales, marketing, and operational efforts must be linked to a common image to be effective. Marketing brochures with pictures of mahogany desks and leather chairs may conflict with a goal of being viewed as the lowest cost provider. Conversely, brochures with employees working at stacked milk-crates for desks may conflict with trying to create an image of high quality and professionalism. Consistency is critical here, and most people understand this concept intellectually if not intuitively. However, there is a strategic

component to positioning as well, particularly when an organization is seeking new markets.

The figure below shows various companies and their relative position in a specific market based on perceptions of product price and quality. The size of the circles reflects the relative size of the various organizations.

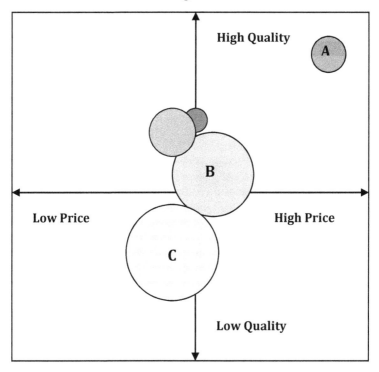

A figure such as this can be used to both identify opportunities in the market or concerns about your organization's current position. For example, if this figure represented a new market a organization was trying to enter, it would appear that there is an opportunity for a high quality, above average priced approach, as there appears to be room between the small organization **A** that is high quality and high priced (upper right) and the large medium quality, moderately priced organization **B** (center circle).

Alternately, it can be seen that two smaller companies (just above and to left of center) are already trying to compete with organization **B** by providing a slightly better product at a slightly cheaper average price. It can also be seen that the largest organization (**C**) competing in this market is viewed as having the lowest quality at a very slight price discount. This large organization has done a good job of maximizing their price, given the competition.

Analyses such as this can be done by organization, or even for a specific product line. Needed is access or a reasonable estimate of the competition's market share and reliable information (preferably customer-based) regarding product price and quality.

The most common mistake companies make in trying to expand is to try to do too many new things at once. They often try to take a new product to a new customer in a new region while trying to develop new skills. It should not be a surprise that failure is more likely than not.

It is important to limit the number of new things you attempt at once. Herein *it is assumed that the only thing changed was the customer.* This is the best way to apply existing skill sets and abilities for growth, successfully. The reader might ask, what if we have totally permeated our accessible markets with our existing products? Ah, then you need new products – which is a totally, and dramatically, different discussion, and a different process called the New Product Development Process. There are many books written specifically about that process so that discussion has been excluded here!

Summary
Using Chapters 8 and 9 as background you should be able to put together a marketing plan that meets the needs of your

organization. It could be as simple as writing down: we need another customer like "X" and to get them we will do A, B, and C. Or it could be a complex plan with details that encompass all three Ms, all 4 Ps and all 5 steps of the messaging process. Regardless, the key is that you use this material to write down your objectives and hold yourself accountable to the process you laid out.

Chapter 10
Operational Systems

This chapter examines "Operations" or Operational systems, with a focus on significant continuous improvement of all aspects of producing and providing a product and/or service. Ultimately, what it comes down to is how do you do what you do cheaper, better, and faster. The objective of this chapter is to give you

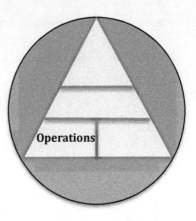

some of the information and tools to make your organization significantly cheaper, significantly better in the eyes of the customer, and significantly faster. First, it is valuable to understand the context within which you are operating.

What phase of life is your organization in?

Every organization has many similarities to an individual, meaning it has a youthful startup phase, a period of consolidation and maturation, and then a phase where growth and diversification are reborn. Sometimes

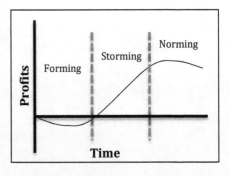

these phases are described as "forming," "norming," and "storming." George Land and Beth Jarmin in their book *Break-Point and Beyond*[33] describe this concept in great detail.

They suggest that the transition between these phases can be very stressful, generating what are called crises or "breakpoints" in an organization.

It is important to know what stage your organization is in. Is it still in the early (forming) phase, when entrepreneurship and risk-taking are critical? Or is your organization getting increased pressure for standardization, consistency, and lower prices (norming)? Lastly, is your organization starting to diversify, to increase employee empowerment, and to seek profitability through wide specialization (storming) rather than commodity production? It is extremely important to recognize that *each of these phases (forming, norming, and storming) requires a significantly different approach to leadership.* Risk-taking entrepreneurs are not generally good at managing issues such as consistency, repeatability, and reliability. At the same time, leaders who are experts at these three skills are often uncomfortable with the sharing of power, loss of control, and creativity necessary to move to the specialization and diversification of the storming phase.

It is also important to recognize it is common for organizations to get stuck in one of the three phases for years and even decades! This is simply because the leadership needs of the three phases are so dramatically different, and in many ways the opposite of what is needed in the previous phase such that the change appears risky when it is actually essential. To truly continuously improve, it is important that you objectively evaluate which phase your organization is in, and your leadership skills as they apply to that phase and the next. Often, when an organization is struggling, it is because they are trying to move between phases but lack the internal leadership skill sets to do so. Usually, new leadership skills (and often new people) are required.

What phase of life are your products or services in?
Not only does your organization go through a maturation cycle, but your products do as well. The most common discussion on this topic generally revolves around the "Product Life Cycle" graph.

This graph shown below is discussed in detail in introductory marketing books, so little time on is spent on this topic here. Nonetheless, it is important to understand that each product goes through a series of phases in the marketplace from *introduction*, with little or no profit, to *growth* with high profitability, to *maturity* with its higher volume but generally lower profitability per unit (or percentage), and finally to the *decline* phase with increasing competitiveness, and smaller margins.

Product Life Cycle Stages

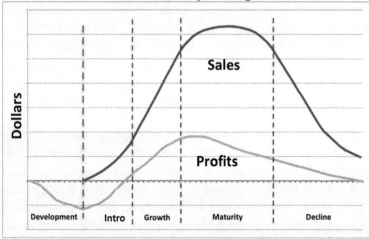

An organization needs to recognize where their product(s) are on this graph, and to do everything in their power to keep all their products [34] from ending up in the decline phase. With appropriate strategies it is possible to regenerate growth in a product or service that has entered the mature or decline phase. Alternately, judicious introduction of new products avoids having all products in any one phase. Both these approaches assume that it is known which phase each product or service is in and that strategies are being created to optimize performance based on that knowledge.

It is not uncommon, particularly in manufacturing, for leaders with specific kinds of skills to freeze their company and all their products in a particular development phase (accidentally or on purpose) for years on end and suffer a slow attrition of profits rather than adopt (or hire) new leadership skills that are unfamiliar and perhaps counter to their previous experience.

Naturally, the phase that products and/or services are in and the phase an organization is in are linked. The greater the variety of products/services offered and the greater the variance in where those are in their life cycle the more important communication and facilitation (and shared leadership) skills become.

Evaluating Operational Subsystems

Once an objective understanding of the context you are operating in has been gained, you can begin evaluating your Operational System for improvement. In reality, the overall Operational System is made up of many smaller systems, and each of these

Each System and Subsystem is either the purpose of a position or a major responsibility of a position – depending on the size of the company and the system.

smaller systems is either a major responsibility of someone or the actual purpose of someone's position - if the activities are sufficient to warrant it. Common subsystems of Operations include:

- Purchasing

- Inventory
- Manufacturing
- Quality
- Shipping and Receiving
- Costing (sometimes included in financial system)
- Maintenance
- Process Improvement (E.g. R&D, LEAN)

Each of these subsystems may have further subdivisions, depending on the size and nature of organization. For example, manufacturing can be divided into a number of processes. A process in this case is defined as: "a series of actions that produce something or lead to a particular result" (Merriam-Webster). Example manufacturing processes include:

- Manufacturing
  - Cutting
  - Shaping
  - Boring
  - Moulding
  - Finishing
  - Assembly
  - Packaging

The purpose of each process is to add value, *as defined by the Marketing System*. The purpose of Process Improvement is to eliminate activities that do NOT add value, as defined by the marketing system. This latter purpose is the primary focus of many LEAN activities.[35] Common activities that do not add value include material handling and waste management. Although these may be important to the organization, they do not add value in the customer's eyes.

Communicating System Improvement

All communication about process improvement should be consistent, as poorly communicated activities can easily appear to be in conflict with each other when people are trying to implement them. Thus a system for prioritization is very handy. One such system I refer to as the **S**afety, **Q**uality, **S**ervice and **P**roductivity (**SQSP**) approach. This approach integrates the concepts of the right product (Quality), at the right time (Service) at the right price (Productivity) with the overarching organizational objective of a safe working environment (Safety). Thus this is not only a categorization of activities for discussion, it is a prioritization sequence. First you do things safely, then you do them right, then you do them on time, and then you do them productively (cost). By consistently discussing operational activities in this manner, in this order, you create a culture that values all four components. The people in the organization know that you put them first, and money last, but that all four are critical to both their and the organization's success.

The secret to lasting process improvement is clearly defining overarching long-term goals that improve your ability to provide value to the customer greater than that provided by a competitor. Collins and Porras in their 1994 book *"Build to Last: Successful Habits of Visionary Companies"* proposed the concept of Big Hairy Audacious Goals (BHAGs) as a way to focus the organization's effort. BHAGs should be clear, compelling, and a clear catalyst for team spirit.

Good, BHAGs commonly include:
We need to…

- Improve the safety of our facility monthly and thus be able to decrease our insurance modifier by 20% (**S**)
- Precisely measure, and meet our customers exact requirements (**Q**)
- Cut our reaction times in half (**S**)
- Grow sales per employee by 10 percent (**P**)

- Be intimately aware of our customers wants and needs (both spoken and unspoken) in order to help them do what they do better

Implementing SQSP

Safety:

Safety is a great place to start the continuous improvement process, because it can have such a broad impact on all parts of the organization. For example, by gathering a list of all the things the employees' feel should be improved for safety reasons, you generally get a feel for specific activities that are repetitive and wasteful such as material handling. By addressing those activities specifically, you not only reduce handling but also garner employee support for continuous improvement in general. Also, if you post the list of requested improvements, including all minor ones, you are able to cross things off the list regularly thereby visibly demonstrating safety is a priority and employee concerns are being addressed. Traditional safety committees can manage the activities to address requested improvements within the organizational budget.

Quality:

Contrary to popular belief, "high quality" means providing exactly what the customer expects and is willing to pay for, nothing less and nothing more. The importance-performance analysis discussed in the marketing chapter is the basis for defining "all things better." It is a common misperception and in some cases a tragic error to believe your competitive strength lies in "exceeding" your customer's demands. *Your competitive strength should be to exceed your competitor's ability to exactly meet your customer's demands.* Below is an example of how a value gap in product performance can develop over time.

Value Gap Example:
Company X is proud of their ability to exceed their customer's expectations, and they strive at every opportunity to improve their product and their service. Over time they have successfully inched both their price and their margins higher based on this approach.

Along comes a new entry into the marketplace. The entry does a careful importance-performance analysis of what the customer really needs. They find that the product that fulfills the customer's core needs has many fewer attributes than currently being provided. In addition, in order penetrate the market the new entry is willing to take a lower margin. The net result is they offer an acceptable product to the customer at a significantly lower price, sometimes as much as 40-50 percent lower. The customer is initially a bit incredulous, and probably excited. The customer share's this info with Company X who is likely taken aback by the scale of the difference in both product and price. As a result, they may become defensive and a common response is either "we don't provide junk" or "our products are far superior and are worth much more." What they may fail to see is that the difference in price now outweighs the benefits from the superior product. Often, company X loses the customer.

Yet experience and interviews indicate that companies like X could have provided a similar product to that of the competition for similar or only slightly more than what the competition offered, and done so with less risk for the customer... i.e. they could have kept the customer.

In the above example, what Company X could have said was, "*we can be much cheaper as well if you are truly comfortable with a product like the one the new vendor is offering. In addition, we are willing to work with you to continue to provide a high level of service and find a compromise that still gets you a much cheaper product without sacrificing our relationship and risking unreliable performance for your customers."*

In the latter case they probably would have kept the customer. Interviews with customers that have switched suggest that most would have paid more to stay with an existing known, and reliable supplier. The point here is simply to emphasize the fact that the goal is to provide the customer what they want and need, no more no less.

The list of details of what the customer expects and wants is generally referred to as product specifications. The more detailed you are in defining product specifications the more precise you can be in meeting them. The *Quality* subsystem is generally charged with defining how precisely the organization is meeting the customer's specifications. Thus in any organization that provides a product or service, someone in the organization should be responsible for measuring, tracking and reporting performance against customer expectations.

> *To meet the varying and highly specific demands of its OEM customers one secondary manufacturer of maple wood products came up with 20 shades of "white maple" to help clarify and consistently meet customer expectations.*

Generally the person responsible for quality also tracks things such as:

- On-time delivery (based on customer expectations)
- Rejects and returns
- Waste
- Yields

More sophisticated organizations track reasons for various occurrences, such as why a product was late, why it was rejected, or what characteristic caused it to become waste. Improvements need to be based on actual data rather than intuition for them to be successful.

Service:

Good service is dominantly about the ability to react quickly to a customer's needs. To a certain extent the process of *figuring out how to produce things faster is the best BHAG* an organization can adopt. Faster is generally defined by lead times that are easily measured in the marketplace and short lead times can become a clear competitive advantage. But the ability to respond quickly is equally important to your organization. An organization that can react within 24 hours, even if they officially have a two-week lead-time to the customer will likely never have a late order. They can (and should) also charge a premium for expedited orders that actually incur no additional cost. Finally, and perhaps most important, the ability to produce things quickly and accurately allows you to increase the sales volume you can put through the organization's facility with a given overhead. This leads to significant improvements in profitability.

In general, reducing lead times in half is a common major goal and one that can continue on for years as successive improvements get harder and harder to attain and have more and more value to the organization.

Recognition that all lead times are based on a series of increasingly refined estimates or forecasts is critical to shortening lead times. You just have to control the things you can and not worry about those you can't; and limit variables wherever possible. Sometimes you even sacrifice yield in the name of reducing the number of variables you are managing and to shorten response time, and thus the ease of on-time performance. In general, to refine your forecasts you must recognize the closer you get to an actual order, the higher the predictability of the content of that order. In theory, once you get an order it is 100 percent predictable as to content. However, experienced business people know that in some businesses change is commonplace, and even actual orders may only be 95 percent "real." Overall, you want to differentiate between the things you can know and manage and those you can't; and not let the unknown keep you from planning or leading to inaction.

How do you make Big Hairy Audacious improvements in lead times? An example[36] may be helpful:

A company producing a custom cabinet has a 4-5 week lead-time. The BHAG is to reduce this to 2 weeks. There are two major components of this lead-time, design and manufacture. In general the final design process takes 1-2 weeks and the manufacture takes 2-3 weeks.

To reduce design time you need to create a clear structure for the design process and share that with the customer. Basically this is an, "if you do this we will guarantee this" approach. This structure should focus on documenting major decision points and times they need to occur to achieve the desired lead-time.

To reduce manufacturing time you need to a) restrict the start of manufacturing processes until the order is fully defined, b) apply Mass Customization principles to your component mix, c) apply LEAN principles to the production process and d) implement Vendor Management programs that guide your make or buy decisions with your vendors. Mass customization allows you to maintain an inventory of component parts (e.g. sides and backs of cabinets) that are relatively interchangeable for a majority of your products. LEAN helps you prioritize and speed materials through the process. Vendor management processes allow you to source materials or components from their inventories on short lead times for 80 percent of your projects.

Productivity:

The concept of Productivity is directly linked to the benefits that the customer values and is willing to pay for. Thus, the importance-performance analysis discussed in Marketing

Always use actual variable expenses to analyze and plan cost savings activities.

System is critical for operations to have a clear understanding of where to focus. Basically you reduce or eliminate activities the customer does not value.

Most companies are pretty comfortable with the concept of being productive, and establishing goals of making their processes much more efficient, but not with the implementation of significant change. This is often because there is a lack of either an analysis of the various costs of production or the data/information needed to do that analysis. Intuition can be both valuable and deadly when trying to do a relative cost analysis in operations. So the first thing an organization may need to do is figure what they want to know, and gather the data to figure it out. In gathering data for cost improvement is it critical that that data be "pure." By that is meant the use of actual direct expenditures rather than "burdened" or "process-weighted" costs. This topic will be discussed in more detail in the Financial Systems Chapter, but for purposes here a brief example is provided.

It is also possible, and not uncommon, to incorrectly leave highly efficient (E.g. CNC) equipment unused because work center burdened labor rates for that equipment suggest it costs $75-$150/hour to operate it versus $35-$50 for less automated versions. In reality, the pure cost is often less than a $5 difference, based on skills of the operator; and the more automated equipment usually does a faster, more accurate job.

137

Companies often determine the cost of labor by calculating an average hourly rate for workers including all benefits and all other overhead costs. This is called a fully burdened labor rate. This approach is important in many situations, but not in cost reduction, because a savings in direct time of personnel has no impact on most overhead expenses (e.g. rent, depreciation, taxes). In fact using fully burdened labor data usually concludes that reducing the number of personnel increases the labor rate per hour, thus masking the benefits of the improvements. So, you can incorrectly aim at the wrong activities and potentially misrepresent cost savings. The easiest way to address this is to simply use actual average wages for a given position plus payroll taxes and benefits to calculate labor savings - and historical averages of other actual variable expenses for all other costs.

In most situations cost savings are based on two simple metrics: labor and materials. So once you have an accurate measure of current labor expenses per process (from your data gathering) and historical averages of material expenses, you have a basis for setting goals. In general, these are two different issues but can be approached concurrently – as they affect each other. Thus each year you want to establish improvement goals for both materials and labor, but improvement in gross margin is the overarching objective.

Materials: The single biggest cost category for materials is inventory! By far!! In general, accounting studies over the past 50 years have shown that the average annual EXPENSE for inventory equals approximately 25 percent of your average annual inventory. That is, for every $100 thousand in inventory you have it costs you about $25 thousand per year in actual expenses to have that inventory. So a $4 million average inventory costs you about $1 million per year to have.

Now this expense rate (the 25 percent) does vary a bit, generally from a low of about 15 percent to as much as 40 percent depending on business and economic climate. But a rule of thumb of 25 percent has proven to be VERY accurate over the past 30 years in particular. How can this be true? This inventory expense includes cost of:

- Capital
- Storage
- Handling
- Mishandling (damage, incorrect product shipments, returns, reorders)
- Mis-order (too much, too little, wrong thing)
- Old or distressed inventory
- Excess Work In Process (WIP)

This expense would even be higher if you considered lost opportunity cost, i.e. the opportunity to invest the money tied up in inventory into process improvements (including marketing) and capacity expansion. Thus, reducing inventory is one of the highest priorities of the organization and you can usually afford to pay more for just-in-time delivery of product, although in practice additional costs are often minimal! *So each year set big inventory reduction goals* (measured in total inventory, inventory turns, or similar).

After cost of inventory, material costs vary greatly by organization, but the next big category tends to be material yield. Costs due to yield loss are generally related to:

> REMINDER:
> Even though we are referring to "systems" here in the discussion, in small and medium-sized companies these systems are generally part of one person's job, and thus their individual goals!

- Process efficiency (e.g. speeds)

- Process control (e.g. manufacturing defects)
- Quality standards (agreement on what's acceptable)
- Material optimization capabilities (how much you purchase versus use)

The second annual goal for materials is generally for yield improvements. Note: trying to buy the material at the most effective price would primarily be part of a different sub-system, the Purchasing system.

Labor: A great focus for labor improvements is in those tasks that staff report to be "wasteful" or physically difficult (or even painful) to do. Often these are material handling activities. Many companies have found that by simply asking employees what tasks they find painful or wasteful or even dangerous, they end up with a list of process improvement activities that both the organization and individuals are motivated to resolve; and have a big impact on performance. Also, by starting with the employee list of improvements and addressing those first you begin the process of *creating a culture of continuous improvement.*

The creation of a culture of continuous improvement is critical for the long-term success of activities such as the implementation of practices such as LEAN. The idea behind LEAN is to "maximize customer value while minimizing waste.[37]" The fundamental goal behind LEAN is to create more value for customers using fewer resources. Researchers from MIT coined the term LEAN in the 1980s based on their investigation of the successful practices of Toyota. Although LEAN is often linked with manufacturing, it actually applies to every organization and every process. Jim Womack and Dan Jones discuss LEAN characteristics in detail in the book "*Lean Thinking.*" LEAN thinking has impact on all the three major strategic objectives (Cheaper, Better, Faster), but generally a starting place is the optimal coordination of people (labor) to achieve significant improvements in material costs, inventory, and lead times.

Experience (and some research) suggests that many American companies tend to apply LEAN practices without fully adopting the LEAN Thinking approach; and thus generate fewer, less consistent and less lasting overall benefits than many of their foreign counterparts. For this reason I generally recommend you first create a culture of continuous improvement within the organization and then bring in LEAN as a process or system to help achieve organizational goals. This is the main reason I include this discussion in the labor section of improving operational systems.

It should be noted that clear and agreed on work instructions play a critical role in system improvement. The difference between work instructions and job descriptions is that work instructions are specific to a piece of equipment, process, or activity while a job description is specific to a position or person. Thus job descriptions and work instructions work hand in hand, as one responsibility for a worker might be to operate all equipment in accordance with individual equipment work instructions. By defining and aligning how people accomplish tasks it makes it easier to evaluate and improve activities.

A second success factor in achieving labor savings is to ensure that people with the right skills, and pay rates, are *doing the right things at the right time*. To a certain extent this is about internal value-added. That is, having a $25 per hour person (assuming wages are related to specific skills and experience) doing a job that can be accomplished equally well by someone with less skill and experience is a loss of value-added brought by the skilled individual. For example, if two highly skilled individuals (say $25 per hour) spend 20-25 percent of their time doing activities that could be accomplished equally well by a introductory level person (say

141

$15 per hour), then you are losing $10 per hour times 1000 hours per year or about $10,000. The bigger the gap in wages (e.g. the CEO doing minimum wage activities) or the greater the number of hours spent doing these things, the more you are losing.

Similarly, *having the wrong number of people in the organization can be costly.* It is not uncommon for companies with highly seasonal businesses to experience large overtime premiums during the busy seasons. Average workweeks of 50+ hours are not uncommon; and often the highest paid employees work the longest hours. There are many seemingly good reasons to address seasonality this way, including lack of a pool of trained employees, but there is a very high cost to this approach. The example on the next page highlights the loss incurred by failure to address excess wage payments.

This is not to say that addressing seasonality is easy, but that it is VERY important. All too often addressing overtime becomes exclusively an equipment issue rather than creatively identifying human resource solutions as well. The next chapter offers some suggestions and tools for addressing highly seasonal labor demands. These are not the only solutions to reducing labor and material costs, but may be new ways to look at the big possibilities.

Annually documenting areas for improvement in your operating system and the actions you can take to achieve those improvements is the basis of the operations plan. The operations system is focused on coordinating and optimizing resources, including people. The result of a good system is happy customers and a happy organization.

Company Z has 50 shop employees with wages averaging $16/hr. for 80% of the staff and $25 per hour for the top 10 highly experienced and skilled individuals. In addition they have highly seasonal sales, with 50% of sales occurring in 3 months. During the busy times everyone works an average of 50 hours per week except the 10 highly skilled people that tend to work 60 or more.

In busy times they pay an overtime _premium_ of:
40 people x $8/hr. x 10 hours overtime x 13 weeks or $41,600 – PLUS
10 people x $12.50/hr. x 20 hours overtime x 13 weeks or $32,500 for a total of $74,100

At 600 hours of overtime, the 50-person organization is effectively short 15 people. That is, <u>15 more people, at an average wage of $17.80 during that period would **save** them the premium of $70,000</u>. (Note: suppose the company does $5 million in sales so this reflects more than 1% of revenue. They also have a pretax profit of 3%, or $150,000, so even a savings of half, or $35,000 would be a almost a 25% improvement in profits!!)

Chapter 11
Financial Systems

Many companies base all their financial reporting either exclusively for tax reasons, or for reporting to their bank, or both. Yet the primary driver of financial reporting should be to meet the needs of the organization, not these outside factors. This doesn't mean that you do not do reports specifically for banks

or governments, but it means that your highest priority should be to develop the financial reporting that allows you to best understand what it going on in your own organization and to guide you in making changes to improve. It is also to recognize that certain financial indicators developed to guide one kind of evaluation may hinder or even mislead decisions on other issues or in other situations.

The purpose of this chapter is not to teach you to be an accountant nor is it to guide you in calculating taxes or making investments. You need advice from experts specific to your situation to address those issues. The purpose of this chapter is to guide you in the simple running of your organization and in making every day decisions about how you are really doing and determining the kinds of things you can do to <u>improve your profitability</u>. The way you measure yourself financially can significantly influence that ability.

A CEO once said, "fundamentally we need people to sell stuff and people to make stuff – and everyone else is here to support them." To a certain extent this is true in how you should measure your financials as well. You need to measure the efforts to get sales and the efforts to provide the things that are sold – and these are very separate activities. And the amount of money left over after you have accomplished these activities is available to cover the support infrastructure – or overhead. Thus, the approach shown below is highly recommended as a way to prepare a *profit and loss summary* statement for privately held companies of all sizes.

You want each line on financial reports to be as "pure" as possible. That is, you want these lines of income or expense to be actual values not calculated through some formula. This is similar to how you would do when calculating a cash flow statement. So the following definitions apply:

Sales/Revenues – include all payments from outside organizations to your organization, including freight reimbursements. The only exception would be any income from corporate activities, such as selling shares, equipment or real estate that would be accounted for in the "Corporate Expense (income) line."

Selling & marketing expenses – includes all expenditures for the specific purpose of marketing the organization, includes sales personnel, their benefits and any sales incentives.

Freight – includes the cost of shipping goods to the customer, but *not* freight for purchased materials.

Net Sales – is the amount of revenue available to provide products and/or services and to cover overhead. The Net Sales

Many companies find that their gross margins % varies greatly because their cost of freight changes dramatically depending on geographic location of customer. Calculating gross margin based on Net Sales can address this issue!

number is calculated by subtracting: *freight, selling, and marketing expenses* from *total income*. Calculating net sales this way ensures that costs of freight, usually reimbursed for and accounted for, but not margined in the price, do not affect the gross margin percentage (that is - revenue and expense offset each other). Also, by subtracting the cost of attaining sales from gross sales, those costs are less likely to affect operational accountability (e.g. labor and materials) as *gross margins* are more likely to be a consistent percentage of *net sales* by product or by customer. It also makes it easier to be creative in creating sales incentives, as the clear goal is to *maximize the net sales number while meeting gross margin objectives.*

Variable Expenses – include all expenses that vary based on volume. One way to evaluate this is to determine what expenses would remain IF you had zero sales; those expenses would be your fixed expenses and all others are variable. In most organizations the two major variable expense categories are labor and materials.

Variable Labor – includes all personnel expenses related to providing the goods or services your organization offers. This generally includes everyone except for office administration such as any accounting, human resource, or executive personnel. It also includes related taxes (payroll), and any benefits including insurance and incentive systems. It is highly recommended that labor expenses be actual expenses whether based on cash or accrual method of accounting. It is common for companies to calculate labor based on a "burdened" labor rate, meaning it includes facility costs distributed across all personal usually based on total number of man-hours in the factory. This method is appropriate for investment purposes (e.g. evaluating purchase of equipment) but is not appropriate for evaluating operational success, and it can significantly complicate the evaluation process and the visibility of specific expenses.

Variable Materials – includes all materials specifically required to provide the product or service sold. These are materials that vary bases on sales volume and the number of people required in variable labor (e.g. safety equipment).

Total Variable Costs (often referred to as total cost of goods sold or COGS). Total variable costs equal the sum of variable labor and material expenses. In some companies the COGS expense would also include *marketing and selling expenses*. Including selling & marketing expense in COGS makes sense if marketing and selling expenses are a consistent percent of sales and thus do not swing gross margins widely.

Gross Margin Income – is equal to *net sales* minus *variable costs*. Measured as described here it is often called the *contribution margin*. This means the gross margin dollars are the funds available to pay for, or contribute to, fixed expenses. To a certain extent the goal of the organization is to maximize this number, however possible, while minimizing overhead expenses. This contribution margin concept will be discussed further below, as it has an important influence on how you grow sales and go/no-go selling activities.

Example Profit and Loss Summary

Sales/Revenues

Total Income	$1,180,000
Freight Expense	$30,000
<u>Selling and Marketing expense</u>	<u>$150,000</u>
Net Sales/Revenues	**$1,000,000**

Variable expenses

Variable labor	$250,000
<u>Materials</u>	<u>$500,000</u>
Total variable expenses	$750,000

Gross Margin Income   **$250,000**

Fixed Expenses

Rent (also real estate taxes)	$60,000
Interest Payments	$12,000
Depreciation	$36,000
Insurance (property & liability)	$6,000
Facility maintenance	$6,000
Administration	$100,000
<u>Other fixed expenses</u>	<u>$10,000</u>
Total Fixed expenses	$230,000

Operating income   **$20,000**

Other Corporate Expense (Income)	($2,000)
(E.g. sold old fork lift)	
Pretax Net Income	**$22,000**
<u>Allowance for Taxes @ 40%</u>	<u>$8,800</u>
Net Income	**$13,200**

<u>Fixed Expenses,</u> also called "overhead" or "administrative" expenses, are those expenses that do not change materially over the course of the year, under normal conditions, regardless of sales volume. Thus monthly fixed expenses are usually predictable to within a few dollars at the beginning of the year. By calculating expenses this way *it is possible to track*

estimated profitability daily, since you track labor expense (hours) daily and thus all you need do is track materials. You can also motivate teamwork by posting daily, weekly or monthly gross margin targets and celebrating when the fixed income expenses are covered by gross margin dollars for the month. A variety of tools can be used that can include actual dollars or simple percentages. For example, some companies use a bucket for the year that represents the total fixed expenses for the year and fill it up with gross margin dollars each month over the course of the year. When it is overflowing the organization celebrates!

Daily Breakeven Goal = monthly fixed expenses/# working days per month.

More sophisticated companies can calculate, based on historic trends, what percent of annual gross margin is usually generated each month, mark those on the bucket, and

celebrate each time those goals are exceeded. Other companies have used a thermometer or even a tree; anything that represents something your employees will understand. It is a simple way to motivate everyone to help pay the bills!

Although the major fixed expenses are usually rent/mortgage, depreciation, interest, administration, and insurance, each organization has its' own collection of fixed expenses that are specific to their situation.

<u>Operating Income</u> is the amount left after deducting *fixed expenses* from *gross margin* dollars generated. Thus, the goal is to maximize gross margin dollars generated while minimizing total fixed expense, ideally by making fixed expenses a decreasing percent of Net Sales on a year-to-year comparison.

Corporate Expense (income) includes nonoperational or one-time expenses (or income), such as the purchase or sale of equipment, or other property.

Pretax Net Income is the net income of the organization after all organizational income and expenses are included except for government taxes.

Allowance for taxes and Net Income after Taxes are self-explanatory.

Implications for Break-Even Analysis

By defining the profit and loss statement as described above it is fairly simple to calculate break-even and gross margin objectives, and thus to price products or services to customers. It is also easier to decide go/no-go on competitive bids. For example, if you anticipate approximately $200 thousand in annual *fixed expenses* then you need $1 million in *net sales* at a 20 percent gross margin and $800 thousand in *net sales* at a 25 percent gross margin. Thus this also greatly affects your overall marketing strategy, since this same operation needs almost $1.34 million in net sales at a 15 percent gross margin (e.g. commodity items) but less than $575 thousand in net sales at 35 percent (e.g. specialty items) to break even. This is why many companies sell a combination of the two types of products, but also why selling commodity items is historically less profitable than selling more specialized products and services (and why commodity producers focus on selling more, more, more!).

Another benefit to the use of a simple profit and loss statement as described here is that the responsibility for the

In the housing industry is common for sellers of lumber to get margins of 10-15%, while custom cabinetmakers typically get margins of 45-50%.

150

financial performance of an organization can be shared. In fact, it is reasonable to make certain individuals responsible for specific lines in the profit and loss statement. For example, the person responsible for sales & marketing is responsible for maximizing net sales and gross margins based on an anticipated cost.

Marketing Implications

The approach outlined above also makes it easier to value both the marketing process and sales activities in particular. When quoting a new product or new customer, the sales & marketing staff simply take the forecast cost and add the desired gross margin, marketing expenses, and then freight cost. To calculate the estimated sales and marketing expense percentage the annual base marketing expenses (excluding incentives) is divided by total expected sales - included sales as if you got this business; to this you add the incentive rate. *New product sales volume should make total sales and marketing percentages decline.* For example:

	Current forecast	*Forecast with new product*
Gross sales volume	$1,000,000	$1,250,000
Fixed sales & marketing	$60,000	$60,000
Sales incentive rate @1%	($10,000)	($12,500)
Net sales & marketing	7%	5.8%

The price of the new product, based on a projected variable cost (labor and materials) of $3 per unit (piece, ton, board foot, etc.) and with a goal of 25% gross margin, would be $3 divided by 0.75 which equals $4, divided by 0.942 (to account for 5.8% marketing expense) or $4.25, plus actual freight per unit, whatever that is specific to the customer and destination.

Additional marketing investment might be required to attract this customer (e.g. travel), so marketing dollars might go up slightly as well, in which case the fixed marketing expense might increase to $65,000 that would still result in a net decline in sales and marketing expense as a percentage of gross sales ($65,000 + $12,500 ÷ $1,250,000 = 6.2%, which is still less than 7%). This reality is why growing companies can, at least in theory, *lower* their price to ALL their customers and still maintain constant net profit as a percent. That is, the new 5.8% sales and marketing expense percent calculated in example above is true for *all* customers, IF you get the new sales.

This approach also facilitates use of incentives to grow and aim sales activities. So, if you can afford to pay (and are paying) a sales person a rate of $45,000 per year plus a one percent incentive (for a total of $55,000), based on annual sales of $1 million, then you can likely afford to pay that person more if they sell more - and the organization can still grow profits. For example, you could provide that sales person a higher base of $55,000 for the first million and a higher percentage of all additional sales over $1 million (e.g. 3%). Thus the person could make $115,000 if they grew sales to $3 million, *while still significantly increasing profitability.*

The incentive system can be adjusted based on the difficulty of growing sales (e.g. average sales amount per transaction). Creativity can

> Burdened labor rates are generally at least twice as much as actual labor rates. Thus if labor is 1/3 of total labor-and-materials expense (e.g. 25% of net sales and materials are 50% of net sales), burdened labor rates effectively increase perceived costs by 1/3. So, it would appear that a product that costs you $.75 per unit costs you $1.00 and you would clearly turn down an offer of $.83 at a time you badly needed the business and the offer would have helped you break even.

152

also be employed if the sales person's job is primarily to attract large customers and the operations or customer service staff does much of the servicing of that customer. For example you could pay the sales person a bigger percentage (e.g. 3%) of first year sales to a new big customer and decrease that over time as operations or customer service individuals take over the relationship and thus the sales person has time to seek another new customer(s). Clearly you can tie sales incentives to gross margin as well, meaning the higher the gross margin the greater the incentive.

The other critical point related to marketing is how the P&L affects the decision point in determining when to accept an offer on a competitively bid product. By calculating your gross margin as described herein, you can theoretically take any order that has ANY gross margin at all, as long as it doesn't tie up people's time or facility space that would otherwise be generating more money doing something else. So the evaluation is simply about time, space, and opportunity cost. Thus, if business was very difficult, and the example organization was only generating $500 thousand in sales at 20 percent, and the opportunity arose to get an additional $1 million in sales at 10 percent, it would be worth taking as long as it didn't measurably affect overhead costs (meaning it used existing facilities and equipment). This volume would help the organization breakeven (contribution margin of 10% of $1 million plus 20% of $500 thousand = $200 thousand to overhead expenses). The low-margined sales would be even more attractive if there were opportunities to gain efficiencies or sell additional added value over time (thus increasing margins).

Profitability by customer and by product
It is important for the person responsible for sales and marketing to know gross margin profitability by both product and by customer to correctly evaluate those things you want

to do more of and those things you want to do less of. The "weed and feed approach" suggests that you are constantly trying to do more profitable business with more profitable customers while reducing the amount of effort you are putting into low margin activities. Thus financial reports prepared for use to evaluate sales performance should reflect this. By simply using actual labor and actual materials to evaluate individual products, projects or customers, it is just a matter of tracking personnel time and materials used (or a random sample) to estimate margins. This process also aims

Example Profit and Loss Marketing Detail

Sales/Revenues by Customer Category

Customer Category A	$600,000
Customer Category B	$350,000
Customer Category C	$230,000
Total Income all Customers	$1,180,000
Freight A	$6,000
Freight B	$20,000
Freight C	$4,000
Total Freight	$30,000
Selling and Marketing expense A	$70,000
Selling and Marketing expense B	$75,000
Selling and Marketing expense C	$5,000
Total Selling and Marketing	$150,000
	% Net Sales
Net Sales A	$524,000 (52.4%)
Net Sales B	$265,000 (26.5%)
Net Sales C	$221,000 (22.1%)
Total Net Sales	**$1,000,000**

Gross Margin Income	**by Customer Category**
Customer Category A	$131,000 (25.0%)
Customer Category B	$49,000 (18.5%)
Customer Category C	$70,000 (31.7%)
Total Gross Margin	$250,000

the marketing process at the kinds of new products and customers you want go after. Fundamentally you want to go after more sales of the kinds of products that are most profitable or find more customers with the same characteristics as those that are currently most profitable (e.g. you want more of Category C and less of Category B for example in text box).

Implications for Operations

The operations manager is responsible for meeting labor and material expense objectives – generally as a percent of net sales. It is also possible to subdivide labor and materials based on operational systems or processes to provide the operations team the ability to do a more detailed monitoring and analysis of those systems and processes. It also facilitates the ability to have annual and monthly objectives. If clear objectives are not in place it is hard for individuals to be responsible for (or accountable to) them.

To succeed, operational staff needs financial measures that reflect the dominant ways the organization does business. Thus, any subcategories of labor and materials in financial reporting should reflect the major groupings of things you do, either by customer/customer type (if they buy a consistent or similarly produced products) or by product/product group. Groups of products that have widely varying margins from each other, or widely varying processes from each other, should be separated on a financial report prepared for use by the operations staff. In this way factors that may be affecting average margins as the proportions change (i.e. as you sell more or less of a high or low margin product) can be more easily seen.

The process of determining the best way to measure financial aspects of operations can be a bit iterative; that is you may have to try a few options to see which ones work best for you. This activity is inherent in the analytical role of the person doing your financials.

Costing

The success of the operations team is predicated on them meeting or beating projected costs, and on continuous improvements in processes and efficiencies. To accomplish this, the dominant approach for the use of existing equipment and processes is to simply measure actual labor and actual materials used to produce a product, including maintenance. Any consideration of purchase of new equipment MUST consider the effect the cost of the equipment will have on your fixed costs, and thus any effect on needed margins.

This is a very simple and straightforward way to evaluate costs. Of course it is essential to be comprehensive, and consider everyone that actually is required to make it happen. What is required is simply to measure the time and the number of people required to make an individual (or some volume) of product. So, for example if there are 10 people (including supervisor and maintenance) required to make 500 widgets over the course of 4 hours, and the total wages for this group for the 4 hours is $1000 – then your widgets cost $2 apiece plus materials. If it takes $2000 in materials, including any worn tooling, sandpaper, grease and oil, then the total variable cost is $6 ($2 plus $4). The sales staff would then add target margin (say 20 percent in this case), plus marketing expenses, plus estimated freight to get final price.

Of course it may not be as simple as 10 people making this particular product, as you may have parts and pieces made by different departments. But the basic theory is the same… you just have to transfer actual labor and materials along as a material from one part to another. Remember, product handling is generally a labor cost as well, as is shipping and processing.

Once these base costs are created it is possible to track actual performance against them to evaluate the operations team. The goal as an operations team is to improve both consistency (and thus predictability) and efficiency. From a financial analysis perspective it is actually better to be predictable than cheap, at least initially. Then labor efficiency (generally reducing product handling and other non-value added activities) and product throughput can be optimized to meet needs of customers.

Inventory

It is important for a successful operations facility that provides a product is to minimize inventory. The financial challenge for most companies (i.e. those that use their inventory as collateral to borrow money from the bank) is that inventory appears to be valuable and provide cash flow. Yet the opposite is actually true. A good rule of thumb is that 25 percent of average annual inventory value is spent in handling, storing, damaging, and financing of that inventory. Also, inventory ties up capital that could otherwise be used for better means. Often the biggest impact leaders can make on material cost is to reduce inventory. For every $100,000 in inventory there is likely a $25,000 per year expenditure incurred. High inventories also reduce flexibility. Instead of great inventories great relationships are needed with vendors. Generally, for less than a 5-10 percent premium (and often none) 25 percent of costs can be eliminated while increasing flexibility.

People often justify old inventory by saying, "we have the space anyway" without considering the impact on handling, damage, and operational efficiencies.

Valuing Inventory

The cost of inventory is also tied to its value. If work in progress (or WIP) is being carried, this is likely also being used to finance the organization – so there seems to be a benefit in valuing this material as high as possible in order to get the greatest loan value possible. However, IF you are using the batch system (which is generally what creates WIP) and/or are managing your processes by emphasizing machine efficiency, you are likely creating excess and in some cases, depending on the number of SKU's you have, this excess is produced every month. Then that inventory gets highly valued (since you added a lot of effort into it), put into storage, and potentially thrown away, written down, or sold at a significant discount a few years later. This process incurs high hidden and unnecessary costs.

There are also products known as secondary and tertiary products. In base industries such as steel or wood products, there are primary products (the main ones you are using the material to manufacture), secondary products (those purposely produced out of the rest of the material and accumulated for expected orders), and tertiary products (those for which there is no specific intended use but something that could possibly be used to make salable products out of later). In general, primary products and secondary products should share the full economic burden of material costs, and the full added costs of processing. Tertiary products should be valued at either zero or as a simple proportion of actual raw material based on the relative quality or market value. As an example, in the wood products industry linear rips of lumber with no specific intended use are often retained in inventory for years at a value proportional to their original cost and volume, in the hope an order will come up that needs them; but they have little real actual value. The truth is, that for many materials, even though processing labor is added to the material, its intermittent form has little or no value – and in reality less than the material you started with. The inventory costing system should take this into account so you don't end up accumulating inventory on your balance sheet that looks good on paper but is worthless if you actually had to sell it in any reasonable period of time. There is also an economic cost to handling and storage of these materials – so they actually increase in cost over time while decreasing in value. Generally, your best decision is to eliminate these materials from your inventory at a judiciously speedy rate, and certainly within the year.

Productivity Incentives
Productivity incentives, based on individual work center, full plant, or anything in between can be a great motivator toward addressing inefficient operations. In general, the broader they are measured the longer they tend to be valuable. Incentives based on individual work centers tend to lose their motivational impact after a fairly short period of time and become part of the expected pay.. Also, narrowly focused productivity incentives can encourage competition at the expense of coordination and collaboration between processes, resulting in increased efficiency in the detail but reduced efficiency for the whole.

However, short-term incentives can be very valuable even for individual work centers. Staff are usually very comfortable with short term incentive programs when they know they are short-term up front, e.g. for the next two months we are going to provide a bonus if we can get our productivity up by 20 percent. Long-term, broad productivity incentives such as for productivity of a whole office or whole factory can be very useful and motivating.

It is important that the financial system measures productivity accurately and is not rewarding activities that lead to negative behaviors, e.g. a consulting firm rewarding the office if the total billing hours for the month exceed some target has been known to cause "padded" billing activities, that may be good for the month but hurt client relationships in the long run. In general, the old saying, "be careful what you reward, because that is exactly what you will get" is completely true. One way to address this is through "gainsharing," a form of profit sharing discussed below.

Pace of Sales versus Operations

A primary role of financial reports is to guide the optimization of sales volume and operational performance – or flow of the organization - in order to maximize profitability. There are critical high profit points where existing overhead capacity/capability is maximized to produce the volume of sales, and that in order to grow sales volume further you need to increase overhead expenses. Overhead expenses tend to increase in jumps rather than incrementally; it's in their fundamental nature. Thus it is critical for the financial system to identify current peak profit performance such that as you approach optimal sales volume you can make a conscious choice to either grow your overhead expenses, recognizing that this will decrease profitability for a time, OR alternately, refocus marketing activities on shifting sales to more profitable products and or customers rather than higher volume. This activity is basically the pacing role of the financials. You can lose money by encouraging or even incenting sales staff to grow sales of same margin products or services at a time when your overhead (space, support people, etc.) is, or nearly is, maxed out. Thus financial reports should act like a thermostat that you turn up when you need sales and turn down when you want to slow volume growth down or re-aim at different markets.

Forecasting

It is critically important to forecast your financial performance for at least the next year, if not the next five years. This is not to say you should expect this to perfect. The role of the forecast is to provide a kind of rhumb line for financial performance. On a map, a rhumb line is a navigational term for the shortest distance between two points. In reality, you never actually follow that line – but the objective is to get to the end point with minimal amount of effort. The same is true in finance. A financial forecast is simply an estimate of the straight path to your financial goals. You rarely actually follow a forecast exactly, but similar to a rhumb line in navigation the financial forecast helps you recognize when you are straying off course.

To forecast for the next year, the simplest approach using the P&L format included here is to just look at the recent 5 year history for sales volume, add any growth (or shrinkage) expected for each major sales category, calculate labor and materials by estimating gross margins by major category (based on five-year average or weighted by recent trends) and then estimate total gross margin dollars expected. You can then add in actual expected overhead expenses (which should be very accurate) and calculate anticipated profitability. From this you can then determine what kinds of activities you want to encourage to maximize profitability (e.g. pacing and efficiencies). Financial performance should be compared monthly to forecast and activities adjusted to keep the organization on track.

Forecasting Investment – based on depreciation

Depreciation is often one of the largest overhead expenses. Simply put, depreciation is the proportion of a capital purchase (e.g. computer, piece of equipment or building) that is estimated as "used up." All capital assets have what are referred to as "useful lives" which, in the U.S. are based on Internal Revenue Service guidelines. Generally, an organization has assets that are being added and subtracted from the depreciation list each year. Items coming off the list are past their useful lives for tax purposes (they still may be useful assets) and ones added to the list are new purchases. Thus, one way to forecast a base capital budget is by using the dollar amount of depreciation that is coming off the list and multiplying it by the average useful life of the kinds of things you are generally buying (or by proportioning it by a range of useful lives). Thus if depreciation is going to go decrease by $10,000 and the average life of the kind of equipment you tend to buy in a year is 7 years, then your capital budget for the year that will roughly maintain current depreciation expense is $70,000. Obviously there is a lot more thought that goes into capital purchases than this, and this doesn't account for specific needs or access to financial capital to actually make the purchase. But it does give you a starting point for discussion and budgeting purposes.

Profit sharing

Profit sharing refers to the various direct (e.g. paid to individual) and indirect (e.g. paid to individual's 401-K) incentive or financial reward programs that are dependent on the profitability of the organization. There are a lot of tax and financial planning issues that are tied to profit sharing, and it is not the purpose of this book to discuss those. However, one profit sharing program often referred to as "gainsharing" acts as a direct incentive to employees for improving profitability and is generally paid out as incurred, that is quarterly or even monthly under certain conditions. Gainsharing deserves extra consideration as it can tie all employees to the common goal of making the organization more profitable.

Gainsharing

The concept behind gainsharing is that you set a minimum financial goal and reward the employees for exceeding that goal. Your goal should be based on the current needs of the organization and the reward should be as timely as possible to have the greatest effect. To make gainsharing a fair measurement of organization performance it may be necessary to adjust certain financial reporting parameters. The example below provides an example of one possibility for utilizing gainsharing as a profit improvement strategy.

As an EXAMPLE:

Company Q was a manufacturing company with 150 employees and an average Pretax Net Profit of about 3%, which was sufficient for the owners but insufficient for new investment and meaningful profit sharing with employees. They used an individual productivity incentive for years to improve performance and achieve that consistent profitability. But improvements plateaued quite a few years back and they decided to shift to a monthly gainsharing system. Based on industry standards, their own projected needs, they determined that they could share 50% of monthly Pretax Net Profit above 6%, as long as both monthly and YTD profits exceeded 6%, and up to a maximum profit sharing of 20% of regular pay for that month(based on total pool of payroll for the month). So if the Pretax Net Profit above 6% for the month was $100,000 and the total regular payroll for the month was $1 million dollars, everyone would get a 5% (half of $100,000 divided by $1 million) bonus payable the third week of the following month. They implemented the plan.

To make it easier to track and align with hourly payroll they decided to measure periods of weeks rather than months, with each quarter having two four week periods and one 5-week period to align with the calendar. They also decided to go with weekly paychecks at a small cost, which eliminated splitting payroll on 5-week periods and was very popular with employees. Then they set up a plan to attain the profitability and engaged employees in a comprehensive continuous improvement process to help make them more competitive in the market place; shrinking lead times from 6 weeks to one, eliminating 90% of inventory, and improving on-time and quality performance. Every employee became engaged in making the customers happy and saving the company money. Each month the company reviewed performance in detail with all employees to celebrate successes and point out areas for improvement.

It wasn't until the second year that they paid their first monthly gainsharing checks. However, at the end of the first year they were able to give the highest annual profit sharing in history due to improved profitability. The business was highly seasonal, so it wasn't until late summer of the second year that both monthly and year to date profitability exceeded the 6% target. Within four years they were paying monthly gainsharing checks at least 9 months of the year, with a number of the months maxing out at the 20% cap – meaning in a five week period it was like getting an extra week's pay.

As mentioned earlier, linking employee success to overall organization performance and being clear and reasonable about improvement possibilities and individual expectations can lead to great success. It is also important to be transparent and to address any arbitrary reporting methods that can skew performance during the payment period. The shorter the period the greater the motivation, but the more you have to plan for and address specific expenses. For example, if you want to pay gainsharing monthly based on profits it is not fair to employees if profits for that month are affected by a large annual insurance premium payment. Therefore large one-time payments are generally planned for and accrued for in the reporting system to address these performance "anomalies."

Gainsharing is not ideal for every organization. However it can be ideal for engaging all employees on a common goal.

Selecting targets that are a stretch but possible is critical; and those targets can adjust over time. For example the organization above could have announced a graduated reward system, starting at 5% and growing to 6% over time. The important point in this example is that the financial reporting system had to flex in a variety of ways to make the gainsharing system work. The financial system had to fit organizational needs, not the other way around.

Summary
Financial reports designed for the tax purposes and to meet the general accounting principles (GAP) used by banks are critically important... to banks and to the internal revenue service. Ultimately, an organization needs to develop the financial reporting system that serves the needs of planning, marketing, operations, and human resources so that the organization can perform at its optimum. Often this means doing things a little differently than they have been done.

Newport Furniture Parts has a state-of-the-art custom furniture manufacturing facility in the "Northeast Kingdom" of Vermont, one of New England's poorest regions. They provide furniture to high-end design and marketing firms nationally.

For many years NFP had a hate-love relationship with their employees... although it was mostly hate. They ended up in a vicious cycle whereby the lack of trained people combined with trying to reduce labor costs drove them to purchase highly automated and sophisticated equipment, at great cost. To address the challenges of people management they tried to eliminate it, thus diminishing the value of employees and demeaning individuals. The result: increasingly unhappy, inflexible people and years of poor performance (late shipments and financial losses). The company became a slave to its equipment.

The solution: Reengagement, reenergizing and putting people at the center of the organization.
The result: Happy people, a flexible workforce, and the highest profits in company history - less than two years later!

Chapter 12
Human Resources: Empowering people

Have you ever heard someone say, "Business would be easy if it wasn't for all the people involved?" That is not an uncommon sentiment today. 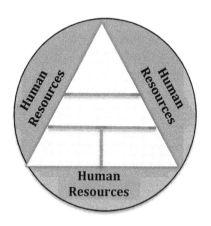 Leading people, with all their quirks and quibbles, beliefs and behaviors, personalities and idiosyncrasies, and faults, failures and foibles can be the bane of leaders of businesses of all sizes. The REAL challenge is that these traits apply equally to the CEO and shop floor individuals alike; let's face it we're all a little crazy sometimes.

So is getting rid of people the answer? That is, should we simply minimize staff through automation and technology? If so, then why do high performing companies like Apple, Google, Netflix, and Patagonia put employees at the center of their business strategies? The answer is simple; business *is* all about people, and it can be valuable to think of your business as a combination sports team and family. You want the best and the brightest on your team, but just like you don't get to choose your relatives, in business you don't always have the perfect choices available. Thus, great leadership and great companies build both from within, and without. They train and develop the people they have and they always keep their eyes open for all-stars.

The Human Resources system (HR) is the communication-hub of the organization. The more people you have, the more extensive the system needs to be. But regardless of organization size, someone needs to fulfill all the functions of HR. In very small companies (less than 10 people) these needs are limited and can either be shared or the top leader does them all. As an organization grows the needs increase as well. Usually by the time an organization has 25 employees the HR activities are sufficient to be about half of a person's position. Some companies outsource these activities and most states have great resources to support companies with their needs, particularly with legal compliance. However, as an organization grows to 60 or more people it is likely that HR is the equivalent of a full time job, and the organization will benefit from a full-time leader of the HR activities.

So, what is HR?
Many companies think of the human resources system as the police department of their organization; it's all about accurate payroll, labor laws and holding people accountable. Although those things are important, the central role of the human resources system (person or department) is to build and maintain relationships with people and to ensure successful communication between the organization and all individuals. At it's heart HR is about ensuring clear expectations, clear agreements, clear accountability, that result in clear outcomes. An important part of that is to identify, attract, train, and retain the people necessary for the organization's success. Additionally, since the success of the organization is linked to the skills of individuals (personal mastery), a key role of the HR system is to create opportunities for the personal development of every individual.

To fulfill the responsibilities of the HR system there a number of important activities or subsystems central to that role, including:

- Posting, clarifying and championing organizational *Vision*
- Communicating how have we agreed to behave – *Organizational values*
- Conflict Resolution – *a critical interpersonal communication skill*
- Clarifying Structure – *Understanding who does what and who reports to whom*
- Clarifying what every individual has agreed to do - *Job descriptions*
- Coordinating performance reviews - *Benchmarking individual performance*
- Defining what individuals get for performing those agreed-upon activities – *Wage, benefit & Incentive systems*
- Establishing employee development programs – *Continuous people improvement*
- Hiring& Firing – *Identifying, attracting, hiring, training, and retaining people that fit the organization's culture*
- Creating labor systems that reflect seasonality – *flexible labor pool including interns, temps, backup positions*
- Developing, maintaining, and communicating employee manual – *clear agreements*
- Minimizing turnover and maximizing employee satisfaction and involvement
- Building relationships between the organization and individuals – *Be a confidant, coach and mentor*
- Assess employee satisfaction
- Provide a support system for employees in crisis
- Provide internal public relations, including "telling the story" of the organization
- Celebration

In short, the human resource system links the needs of the organization and the needs of individuals to achieve a common goal.

Vision and Values

Chapter 5 discussed the process of defining the vision and values. To a certain extent, the human resources system implements the vision and values developed by the leadership team. Usually, the first step is simply posting the vision and values statements where everyone can see them. The second part is in coaching individuals and answering questions related to the value statements. Experience indicates that the first time an organization posts their values statements it will be one or more of the leaders of the organization that will be challenged for their behavior. This is public accountability. If you claim "we" are all supposed to behave a certain way, generally the staff of the organization will be quick to point out any situations where "you" (the leaders and role models of the organization) are not. Thus you must be prepared for this and openly address these challenges. The Mobius communication model described in chapter 1 is an important tool in constructively addressing this situation or "conflict."

Conflict Resolution

Conflict resolution is a critical interpersonal communication skill for people that work together for a common goal. The term conflict in this usage refers to any time two or more people have a different perspective on what is, or should be, going on. Using the situation described above where staff has suggested an individual leader is not living up to, or modeling the values claimed to be important by the organization, the role of the human resources person (or department) is to facilitate resolution of this issue. To do this he or she simply gets the two people in a room and use the Mobius model as a guide. The first question is to the staff person and could be as simple as, "what is missing in this leader's behavior that causes you to believe they are not living up to the organization's values?" It is best if you can get specific situations or examples of behaviors that the staff person didn't feel were meeting the claims of the values. You then ask the leader to define what was missing for them in that situation that caused them to react the way they did.

As an example, the staff person might report the leader yelled at them, which was disrespectful and respect is an organizational value. So missing for them is respect. The leader reports that what was missing for her was trust of the staff person to consistently do things correctly and she was frustrated and thus reacted strongly.

The next step is to define how the situation could have gone differently, and what would have made it more acceptable to both parties. These are the "Conditions of Satisfaction (COS)" within the possibilities step of the Mobius process. In this discussion, there may be multiple missing elements defined, e.g. the staff person says they just don't have enough time or training to do the activity well. The leader might say that she doesn't feel there is enough commitment (based on the definition of trust being: we trust people who show ability and commitment).[38] So then they would clarify what commitment would look like to the leader. Once COS to address what stimulated the behavior are defined, the same thing is done regarding the behavior itself (i.e. the COS for constructive behavior in that situation or situations similar to that are defined).

After all COS are defined, the two parties are asked to commit to change. Basically, answering the question of each party, "If this and that occurs will you agree to behave differently (as described)?" If they don't, then there is a need to investigate further, but in most cases they will and it is possible to move to next steps or actions.

Who does what (actions and responsibility) and by when is next defined, and a point is selected in the not too distant future to get back together (no more than two weeks) to discuss how it is going, with periodic checks thereafter. This later step is the recognition step of the Mobius process, and you celebrate improvement and redo the conflict process where necessary. Generally the issues shrink IF the process of addressing them is begun.

Conflict resolution is a critical skill for all leaders, but especially for the human resources person(s). It is also the number one skill that can be quickly and effectively introduced to leaders for which they get great benefits immediately. Conflict resolution training has at least three components. The first is the process itself, described herein and one that you simply get better with experience. The other two areas involve learning about each other's reactions to stress – a form of *team learning* discussed in chapter 3. Some companies engage all staff members in activities to better understand how and why they react in certain ways to stress. The two common areas for training include conflict style and control dramas.

Conflict style can be measured in a few minutes by a simple test. The Thomas-Kilmann Conflict Mode[39] instrument is available online. The HR person can easily become trained as a test administrator. This conflict style evaluation provides an understanding of people's behavior choices in conflict situations. Five styles are defined: compete, collaborate, compromise, avoid, and cooperate. There is lots of information on-line about these and it is not the purpose of the book to go into them in detail. Most organizations find that testing and discussing the styles of each other within teams, as a group, is a great and fun learning experience. Conflict styles are based on training as well as habit, and will likely adjust due to the learning and support from other team members.

As mentioned earlier, James Redfield uses the term *Control dramas* to describe the relationships defined in Angeles Arrien's book the Four-Fold Way, from which some of the suggested value statements were derived in Chapter 5. Arrien suggests that there are four archetypes or footprints for an individual's reaction to conflict, driven by our experiences very early in life. She refers to these as Warrior, Healer, Visionary, and Teacher with the shadow sides (or negative response) of each being Intimidator, Victim, Aloof, and Interrogator respectively. The discussion of control dramas by Redfield[23] and Arrien[22] offers some insights for helping an individual and teammates better understand each other's reactions to stress, or conflict, and how to help each other to remain constructive. As with conflict style, control dramas can be quickly introduced and fun to learn – especially as a team situation where learning is more easily continued and shared.

Most organizations experience, but don't address lots of disagreement. It is usually just ignored as long as it doesn't get too visible. This creates a culture where hiding feelings and opinions are the norm. Directly addressing conflict minimizes its impact, shortens its effect, and creates an open culture where people learn and care about each other and collaborate to resolve problems and make the organization better. Continuously improving an organization starts with the people and conflict resolution is the interpersonal communication tool that helps people work together effectively.

A word on *gossip* – gossip is an insidious behavior that occurs when conflict is not addressed. Gossip can be defined as any situation where an individual is talking about someone (usually their faults) to a third party when that person is not present. At its worst gossip can result in a divided work force (factions), at best there is an acceptance of and even festering of disagreements that leads to problems later. Yet the solution is fairly simple, though it takes persistence. It is important to recognize that gossip is disrespectful and you don't want it to occur in your organization. So don't accept it. If gossip is occurring and respect is a stated organizational value, address it by pointing out it is important to recognize both speaking and listening to gossip are against organizational values. If respect is not a value... add it. Respect in this usage can be defined as innocent curiosity, meaning that you show up interested in the person and what they are thinking and you assume there is no hidden agenda.

The first step in addressing gossip is to focus on the hearers of gossip even more than the speaker. If people stop listening to gossip it stops occurring. To coach people to stop listening you simply guide them to say to the gossiping person, *"you need to take your issues to the person you are unhappy with. If you need help with that discussion the person responsible for HR can help you – but it is inappropriate for me to listen to you discuss (complain about) someone else."* Make it clear gossip does not align with organizational values, and be persistent, and it will go away. Ultimately you want people to have open, constructive, direct conversations about things that are bothering them so you can address them. To aid this human resources staff can also offer support in communicating differences.

Sometimes people just need to vent to a third party, and it is ok to listen to someone vent as long as you make it clear that is what you are doing and point out that it is a one-time activity. That is, you listen to an issue once and then the person needs to resolve it with the individual they are in

174

conflict with. Again, a third party to help resolve the issue and provide support for communicating differences may be necessary if the gossiping party has concerns about talking directly with person they are unhappy with.

Conflict resolution is a critical interpersonal communication skill for helping people work together. Teams also usually find the training fun and can yield benefits immediately.

Organizational Structure

The organizational structure defines who is responsible for what areas of the organization and who reports to whom. The role of the human resources person is to communicate the structure (in part by posting), to keep all postings current, and to coach all individuals in clarifying their roles. The structure defines the clear lines of responsibility and should empower leaders (and all individuals) to act within their areas with a high level of independence.

The sharing and communicating of the structure helps clarify what is going on from a holistic perspective, and often indicates situations where there is unnecessary duplication or, more often, holes in critical areas, especially as companies grow.

Changing strategic priorities can lead to a need to a change in structure. For example, the determination of whether customer service department reports to the sales and marketing system or the operations system will depend on the annual strategic goals. IF the goal is to significantly improve operational quality improvement, having customer service as part of operations may be an important component of fostering the communication that leads to success. Alternately, if the goal is to enhance the relationship with the customer to expand the range of products or services a customer is utilizing, then the opposite approach may be appropriate. The point is that a structure is not fixed, and may be modified as needed to foster good communication and achieve company objectives.

Just as everyone that is not making or selling something is a support for those that are, the role of leaders as defined in the structure is to be sure those within their area of responsibility have all the resources, training, and skills, to fulfill their roles and meet their responsibilities. To be sure that happens each individual needs clear roles and responsibilities. Written job descriptions insure each individual is clear on what they agreed to do.

Job Descriptions
The basic objective of having job descriptions is to be sure every individual has a clear understanding of their various roles and responsibilities and how they achieve success within the organization. One way to make job descriptions successful is to make them useful – and the primary use of a job description is in the performance review process. Thus creating job descriptions with performance reviews in mind can be very effective.

The best job descriptions include the following categories:
- Position – *the official title of the person in this position*
- Purpose – *a definition of why this position (not person) exists*
- Major Responsibilities – *defined as groups of related tasks that take more than 5% of a person's estimated time annually*
- Percent of time – *estimates the proportion of a person's time they should be spending in each area of responsibility*
- COS – *clearly defines specifically how you would measure success for each responsibility*
- Tasks – *specific activities that address each condition of satisfaction*

A brief example would include:

Position: Operations Manager

Purpose: To ensure the safe, on-time, on-cost delivery of correct product or service to customer

Major Responsibility: To develop, implement, monitor, and adjust activities as necessary to meet the objectives of the annual operations plan

Percent of time: 20%

Example COS:

- Employees report it is a safe environment
- Annual safety goals are being met
- Annual on-time, quality, and productivity goals are met

Example tasks:

- Meet at least monthly with leadership team to coordinate with sales, finance and human resource activities
- Meet with operations team at least weekly to ensure weekly goals are established and resources available to meet them

Each individual should have two to seven major responsibilities. The amount of time to be spent on a responsibility and related COS should be developed by the individual in conjunction with their supervisor and the people they work with.

Each individual and their supervisor should review their job description for

Experience suggests individuals cannot prioritize more than 7 things – and even 7 are a stretch for most people. It is why most ranking systems are from 1 to 5. Therefore keep major responsibilities to a minimum.

completeness and accuracy and formerly agree annually that it reflects what they are supposed to do in the coming year. It should be adjusted as necessary to be clear to both and to meet their individual needs from each other.

You do not need job descriptions for each individual, but rather each position. Thus people doing roughly the same activities can be grouped. In general, EVERY leader has a major responsibility to the people that report to them, to coach, mentor and develop them as individuals and as a group. The proportion of time spent on people issues increases as the number of individuals in an organization increases and with the leader's position For example, a shop floor supervisor may spend 5-10 percent of his or her time coaching and developing staff whereas the CEO may spend 50 percent or more developing leadership staff. In reality, a CEO's success is truly dependent on the development of the leadership team.

Performance Review System

A good job description provides a firm basis for a constructive performance review. Performance reviews should occur semiannually or at least annually to be effective. The Mobius communication tool is again effective process for guiding reviews and avoiding conflict. You simply review those things that are going well (present) and those that could be improved (missing) for each condition of satisfaction on the job description. There are generally many things going well and a few things that need to be worked on. This process should stimulate some good discussion about how things are going. It is also valuable each year to discuss the accuracy and appropriateness of the job description itself and whether it needs updating. You want to agree it is accurate and appropriate (with any corrections) to make the review more effective in the future and with joint ownership in the description.

Performance reviews work best when there are no surprises. That's why it can be valuable to have mini versions quarterly (e.g. 15 minutes), a larger one at the midpoint in the year (e.g. 20-30 minutes) and then the more comprehensive and traditional annual review.

Performance reviews [40] should have two basic components to them, the job description (what you do) and a discussion of behavior (how you do it). Fundamentally this latter topic is about interpersonal communication and how well this person functions within the group. The goal is to have people that function well in accomplishing their tasks and that work well with others; and you want to coach them in both skills.

One way to visualize this is to produce a chart such as that shown below, comparing rankings of people's productivity (how much they accomplish) and a ranking of how well they communicate and get along with others. Some organizations refer to the latter as "living up to the organization's values," since that is ultimately how it is measured.

Stars

If a person is really productive and people really like working with them… people might give that person a ranking of 4-5 for productivity and 4-5 for values (assuming 3 is average with 5 highest, and 1-2 below average). This would put them in the upper right quadrant of the graph below. This would be the kind of person you want to pay attention to, acknowledge and reward. Top performing people are an important asset. Other firms seek out these individuals and, if asked, they often report that the reason they leave is the perceived apathy on the part of their existing employer; that is they didn't feel anyone really cared. The organization may respond they were just leaving them alone because everything was fine.

179

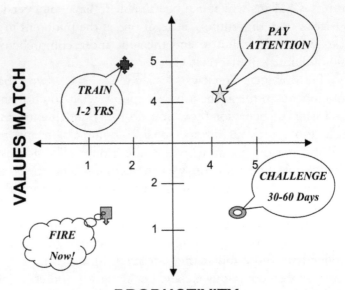

PRODUCTIVITY

These are also the individuals that may get offered a big raise to move to another organization. Studies show that even if the current organization is able to keep the employee after this happens (by meeting pay requirements and other benefits being offered) the person generally leaves within two years. Their trust in how the organization fairly valued them is damaged. So pay attention to (appreciate and celebrate) and financially reward top performers!

People to train or…?
If people report they really like to work with an individual (4-5 on values) but they report this person is below average in productivity (less than 3) putting them in the upper left quadrant, then the organization and the individual need to agree on an individual productivity improvement plan. This can take time, and you can afford to take time to train people

that are well liked, but you want to be clear that at some point in the future you need this person to be more productive.

If people do not like to work with someone (below average on values) but they are very productive they fall in the lower right quadrant. These people can be very disruptive to the organization, and you need to carefully evaluate how disruptive they really are. In general, you do not want individuals in the organization that do not work well with others, regardless of how productive they are. The smooth running of an organization is much more important than the productive attributes of any one individual, and a disruptive individual can seriously effect organizational performance in hidden ways.

It is likely that this person is measuring themselves primarily on productivity and don't value interpersonal issues; and by accepting (and financially rewarding) this behavior the organization has confirmed they are correct. To change this you have to be clear the measurement system has changed and that how you do things is as important as what you do. Some texts even suggest you really have to directly confront[41] these individuals and challenge them to get their attention, especially if these behaviors have been going on for a long time. You must also make change a critical and immediate issue – so the measurement of success must be short term – e.g. 30 to 60 days. In general, these are people organizations fear terminating, but the organizations generally perform more smoothly and more efficiently once they are gone.

Finally, the lower left quadrant represents people with few redeeming features from an organizational standpoint. People report they don't like to work with them and they don't appear to get much accomplished. Many companies have one or two of these individuals in house for one reason or another. Often the excuse is that those individuals have some unique skill or knowledge that the organization fears losing. By addressing what is missing in the organization that this person provides (e.g. transfer the knowledge or define a new source) leaders can begin the termination process. The goal is for these individuals to find a better fit, where both they and the organization can be happier; but they should move on and they should go as soon as possible. It is important to recognize that it is not a service to the individual to keep them employed in a job where they are failing.

Performance reviews are important benchmarks for celebrating individuals, coaching and guiding them to higher levels of success, and developing their skills. Constructive processes tied to clear job descriptions make the review process more effective and more likely.

Wage and Incentive Systems

Most wage and incentive systems develop organically; that is they grow based on the increases and promotions to individuals over time. Very small companies (less than 10 employees) need little structure to pay methodologies. However, as companies grow it is increasingly important that wage and incentive systems become more open and more structured to remain fair. This is not to suggest you don't maintain flexibility and you don't want to put everyone in a box, but you do want to be sure you have clear guidelines that can be used to explain how you decided to pay whom what.

A basic wage system has four core components:
1) Tiered positions
2) Expected high and low wage (range) for each tier
3) Guidelines for how you move up within range of a particular tier
4) Guidelines for how you move up to a higher tier

Tiers: A wage tier is simply a group of positions for which the same pay range can apply. In general most companies can be divided into less than 10 tiers, many less than 7. Supervisors for positions in a tier are paid as part of the tier plus a supervisor premium (e.g. $1.00 per hour). Second and third shifts are also part of a tier plus a shift premium. All shift premiums and supervisor premiums usually go away when people shift times or stop being a supervisor (e.g. go up a tier to a nonsupervisory position).

Ranges: Each tier should have a minimum, starting wage and a maximum top wage for these activities. This range should be based on a market survey of people doing similar activities in similar positions within the same or similar region. Most states and many associations conduct such surveys every year or two. The reason you have a cap is for organizational competiveness. There are some instances where you can pay people a premium to the top end of the market and still remain competitive and successful as an organization. But most companies must respond to market competition and thus are limited a bit by what that competition does.

Guidelines within tier: There should be clear guidelines for how you get higher wages within the range of the tier. These should be based on tangible evidence such as experience, training, ability to do a variety of tasks (e.g. operate pieces of equipment), licenses, communication skills, education, etc. In general, organizations need people with the most flexible skill sets possible, so they can afford to pay people to have a wide range of skill sets and grow within their tier and beyond. Improvements in these skill sets may be position-specific even though the tier isn't. As an example, just because other people in the same tier get a pay increase in their position for getting a fork lift license doesn't mean everyone in the tier can, if there is no need within their position. It still may benefit them in the long run, but it may not in the short term.

Guidelines between tiers: There also should be guidelines for how individuals move up through the tiers. Organizations need backup people for all critical positions for a variety of reasons including growth or someone retiring, so training to enable individuals to move up through the tiers should be encouraged. The skills required for each position should be available to all staff in an open organization.

In general the wage ranges of the various tiers can be shared with the whole staff, but what *individuals* make should not be. An individual can tell others what they make, but the organization does not share personal information such as that.

Annual organization-wide wage increases should be based on market conditions for the ranges (wage inflation) and profitability. Unusual profitability should be paid out as bonuses rather than wage increases.

Incentives are used to reward activities or profitability that varies with volume and is subject to future change. Incentives can be paid monthly, quarterly, semi-annually and annually as needed. The most common incentive program in most companies is for the sales staff, used to spur the identification and attainment of new business. However, incentives can be used to spur all kinds of specific behaviors, including to:
- Gain education (pay for school tuition or seminar attendance)
- Stop smoking
- Recommend a friend that gets hired

- Achieve short-term goals (e.g. re-layout plant within a difficult time-frame or meet quality or service improvement objectives)
- Maintain attendance levels
- Achieve safety targets

Incentives can be money, but do not have to be. Pizza parties, days off, barbecues... any form of fun or reward can be considered an incentive if offered in exchange for some achievement. Some companies even let staff vote on reward, offering a variety of options. For incentives to be successful, people must view them as rewarding, and they are tied clearly and specifically to a measurable accomplishment. It is also important that the objective be viewed as achievable.

Bonuses are often financial incentives, usually tied to achievement of financial goals, but can also be applied to other accomplishments. For example, retaining an important customer that is considering leaving can require significant extra effort on the part of a wide range of people. A bonus can be used in such a case if everything works out. To a certain extent the term "bonus" is often used to describe unexpected rewards. Thus the owner in the example above can incentivize people to retain the customer by telling them they'll get a dollar amount of money if they succeed or the owner can simply and arbitrarily reward (bonus) them for their extra efforts without making a specific promise.

Incentive systems of all kinds are used to reward employees in either unique situations or when the gains are not sufficiently predictable to warrant a permanent change in payroll (e.g. giving everyone a 5 percent raise). As such, incentives are critically important and creative tools that the organization can use to reward staff.

Employee Development Programs

One component of relationship building with staff members is in understanding what each individual desires for their future. One way to do this is to have a simple personal development plan that has long-term and short-term objectives for every individual, for which both the individual and the organization have roles. The idea is that what the organization needs, through the organization's plan and job descriptions, can be tied together with each individual's personal goals and aspirations. There is opportunity to align them to truly motivate individuals and to achieve great organizational success.

Hiring & Firing

Two of the most important moments in an employee's life are the time they are hired and the time they are fired (if that should occur). As such they are very important to the organization as well. When a new employee is hired, history shows that the first 48 hours is critical, and that they may in fact make the determination to stay or not stay long-term based on that first impression. As such it is critical that companies make the entry of a new employee into the organization as positive and valuable an experience, for both parties, as can be done. Employee orientation and initial training (including introduction to the culture) is a role for the human resources person.

Depending on the organization, an employee spends anywhere from the first three months to the first two years with an organization learning their position and thus operating at less than optimal efficiency. Yet most companies remain hesitant to take a couple of days at the beginning to orient the individual to organization practices and culture, in spite of evidence that such activity can make a significant contribution to the employees assimilation rate and long term retention. It is a responsibility of human resources to be sure that the first few days are packed with activities that introduce the employee to the companies practices, culture, employee manual, benefits packages, expectations, opportunities, and simply the everyday life of working as part of the organization. Great HR individuals check in with new staff members, and any direct reports regularly over the first three months or so to ensure they are acclimatizing well and to offer aid when struggles start to occur. A simple meeting plan of meeting with new employees weekly for the first couple weeks, biweekly for the following month, and then monthly for the succeeding couple of months can go a long way to ensuring the organization's investment, and the employee's experience is positive.

Employees deserve a fair and equitable termination (firing) process as well. It starts with the performance review and being sure that any insufficient performance of duties is clearly communicated and documented. Then a written warning system needs to be in place to be used when performance is at a level where termination is a possibility without significant change in behavior. Many companies follow a "three strikes and you're out" policy, meaning the employee gets two warnings and at the third occurrence the employee is released. Regardless of the exact nature of the process, it should be clearly defined and no individual should be surprised when they are terminated.

The HR person or their representative should be present at all performance review processes where a written warning occurs to act as an independent third party. They are there primarily to manage the process, and to be sure all that goes on is clear, fair, and well documented. The HR person should also conduct an exit interview with any terminated person in accordance with organization culture. People-centric companies ensure that a terminated employee is aware of all their options in terms of unemployment compensation and access to public and private support systems to make their transition as easy as reasonably possible. This is all part of a respect closure process for both the lost employee and the remaining individuals, by respecting a person's privacy, feelings and providing support.

Employee Manual
The employee manual documents the vision, values, the procedures, practices and all the policies of the organization. It is also valuable to include the story or history of the organization to give each individual perspective and context. The goal is not to create corporate bureaucracy, but to communicate general expectations clearly and consistently to all individuals. This manual should be updated regularly and signed by employees at time of hire and any time it is materially changed. Some companies customize an individual's version of the employee manual to include specific personal information such as job description, pay and benefits, and any agreements for the coming year such as college tuition reimbursement.

Business Seasonality
The human resources system plays a major role in creatively addressing unique labor needs of an organization such as seasonality of business. Flexible companies with flexible employees are the most successful today, and HR systems that creatively find solutions to a organization's labor planning are critical.

In general, the human resource person needs to be planning a year ahead future needs, to develop both training and development activities for existing staff, but also to identify and attract skilled individuals for short and long-term needs. As an example, one organization found that if they hired college summer staff late in the preceding fall, they could get those individuals to come to training activities either at the winter or spring break, or both, so they were totally prepared for the busy time when they joined the organization at end of the term. In addition, they focused recruitment on first year college students and then if they proved to be good employees, provided incentives to get them to return the following years so that their experience was retained. This is a benefit to both the organization and students needing a job.

The HR person should also look into counter-cyclical businesses to find people that may need seasonal jobs that align with the organization needs. This includes a variety of professions including teachers, but is specific to each location. Developing relationships with these individuals can provide a long-term source of highly skilled individuals that can address seasonal needs.

Partnering with technical colleges, temp services, and state training programs are all part of how a human resource person adjusts and adapts to changing seasonal needs. Creative incentives can also aid in dealing with seasonality. A profit sharing program that allocates funds to employees such that they can afford to take voluntary lay-offs in the slow periods have proven to be effective in some situations. Andersen Window Corporation of Minnesota has a history of having more volunteers for their winter layoffs than they need due to their large profit sharing program.

Seasonality is not easy to address, but a proactive HR program that seeks create partnerships with other organizations can help alleviate financial cost and ensure adequate skills for the organization in all levels of organizational activity.

Relationships and celebration

Studies show that groups that play together are more successful. One important and sometimes-unrecognized role of HR is to champion the recognition, celebration and fun activities of the organization. Organizational picnics are not uncommon and these types of activities should be a regular part of the organization's culture in order to build relationships between individual staff members and between the organization and individuals. These activities do not have to be expensive; potluck lunches with an expanded lunch hour once per month can make a big difference. But consistency and regularity are important.

Great companies also celebrate both the organization and individual's accomplishments. Birthdays, employment anniversaries, and both individual and organizational achievements should be publically recognized and celebrated regularly. Celebrations are especially meaningful when they are personal, contain some story (e.g. history), and are outside of normal procedures. Recognition of everyone doing great things and recognizing accomplishments encourages positive behaviors.

The human resource system in many ways is the most important system in an organization. It is the bedrock on which all human interaction exists, and it can be a partner with all other systems to help people learn to work together to create levels of success otherwise deemed impossible. A good HR person, and system, ensures people are your greatest asset, not your greatest challenge.

Chapter 13
Implementing, Monitoring, Adjusting and Acknowledging

If you have utilized the information in the first twelve chapters you now should have a written plan; and you have communicated it to everyone in the organization. Everyone knows what he or she is supposed to do and what you are trying to achieve. Now, you just need to do it.

A good implementation process is critical to achieving plans. As mentioned previously, the annual plan should be monitored at least monthly by the same team of individuals that developed it. Other teams short monitor their portions of the plan at least as frequently. There also should be regular benchmarks for the intermediate steps that need to be achieved for long-term goals to come to fruition. These benchmarks should be at the core of the monitoring process.

One way to approach the monitoring process is to simply meet each month, review progress toward plan and all benchmarks, and determine what adjustments are necessary if any. Basically, each month you evaluate the previous month, asking the question, "are we on track or not," if so, then "what things do we need to do in the next month to ensure we will stay on track," and if not, "what do we need to do differently to get back on track?"

It is important for you to be proactive about the plan and use it as a map or guide, and not give up just because things aren't going exactly the way you expect them to. There is more than one way to get to a destination if you are clear on where you want to go. If you didn't get the big customer you thought you were going to, then what can you do to make up for it? This implies that you have already discussed backup ideas for all critical situations. But the goal is to develop an organizational persistence toward achieving goals and success.

Buses and Benchmarks

Each morning I take the bus to work, and the stop I choose is about 2 miles from my house, which gives me the opportunity to walk along a lake, commune with nature, and get a little exercise. However, it is an intermediate bus stop, which means if I am not standing there... the bus doesn't stop even if it is a couple minutes early; and the next bus is 35 minutes later. Thus taking the bus is a great lesson in timeliness, time management, and... benchmarking.

Benchmarking is the practice of evaluating and <u>adjusting</u> progress toward a goal. In the case of the bus example, the bus is due at 7:03 am, but generally will arrive between 7:01 and 7:07 – so a reasonable goal is to be there by 7:00...at the latest. To make this happen I know it takes about 35 minutes to make the walk, depending a bit on weather, traffic, wildlife, and, of course, pace. So, I usually plan to leave by 6:25 and don't panic unless it gets to be 6:30.

At the same time I know that over the course of the walk my timing will vary. So I have marked out two points along the way as measures of my progress. First I have a point about halfway, where I say I need to be by a certain time to make the bus stop by 7:00. If not I adjust my pace. Then I have a second location that I need to arrive at by 7:50, or... I'm running.

These benchmarks assure that I don't miss the bus and allow me to enjoy my daily walk. Benchmarks in business work the same way. They allow you to adjust along the way to ensure you achieve the end results you desire.

You always want to regularly communicate to all staff how the organization is doing toward achievement of its goals and objectives. Are we getting there or not? And, if not, then what are we going to do about it? It is a way to hold leadership accountable to achieving the kind of success necessary for a happy and thriving organization.

Summary
The key to success in business is to "think, speak, and do." To accomplish the myriad tasks necessary to significantly improve an organization, a leader needs to:

- Assess the organization as broadly as possible, at least annually, to define opportunities for improvement
- Prioritize those opportunities based on which ones would yield the greatest benefit in the next year (opportunities become possibilities)
- Define what success would look like for each possibility
- Commit to the ones that you can agree on will make the biggest difference
- Put a plan in place to do just that
- Define who is going to do what
- Define successive steps or benchmarks in the process that clearly delineate how the organization is proceeding toward objectives
- Create a process to monitor progress and adjust as necessary to stay on track
- Communicate every step of the way
- Train people to work together to get things done (facilitation, collaboration and conflict resolution
- Acknowledge and celebrate accomplishments

Someone[42] once said, "*The definition of insanity is doing something over and over again and expecting a different result.*" In order to make great change within an organization, you must do something different. To do something different you must often think a bit differently, and usually more broadly. Creating, facilitating, and leading an organization by sharing the leadership role is a proven way to achieve new outcomes and address more issues, more quickly, more comprehensively, and with less stress than going it alone. The tools in this book can guide that process and make success more likely.

Footnotes & References

[1] See, for example: Howe, Jeffrey L: Gephart, John; Adams, Roy. 1995. Identifying the success characteristics of small and medium size manufacturers: a survey of wood products companies in Minnesota. Journal of Applied Technology 8(1): 49-53.

[2] Anonymous

[3] Gandhi - (http://www.brainyquote.com/quotes/quotes/m/mahatmag an105593.html)

[4] Stockton, William; Demarest, Larry; Herdes, Marjorie; Stockton, Joyce. 2004. The Mobius Model: A guide for developing effective relationships in groups, teams, and organizations. 58 p. (http://www.capt.org/catalog/MBTI-Book-60517.htm)

[5] Senge, Peter M. 2006. The Fifth Discipline: The art and practice of the learning organization. New York: Doubleday. 445 p.

[6] Kocolowski, Michael D. 2010. Shared Leadership: Is it time for a change? Emerging Leadership Journeys, Vol. 3 Iss. 1. Regent University, School of Global Leadership & Entrepreneurship. Pp 22-32.

[7] Pink, Daniel. 2009. Drive: The Surprising Truth About What Motivates us. Riverhead Books, published by the Penguin Group, New York.

[8] © Opinegraphics | Dreamstime.com - Mobius Loop Photo

[9] The time period is based on the example of an annual plan that is being used.

[10] For more information on Five Finger Voting see: http://www.iaf-methods.org/node/5105

[11] People often are passive when they have a concern based on intuition and hard for them to articulate. That concern is

important, and asking people to physically respond can get them to speak to fears that can likely be addressed.

[12] Concurrent used in this context refers to same-time interactions such as phone, Internet, and in-person rather than linear communications such as texts and emails.

[13] Discussed further below.

[14] Check-in and Checkout processes often use a "go-round" format, which means you ask each and every individual to respond. The sequence may vary, but you want ALL individual's input.

[15] http://mitleadership.mit.edu/r-mulcahy.php

[16] It can be valuable, and time saving, to give the individual's the present-missing questions ahead of time to think about, although you generally discourage discussion between respondents so that the responses are clearly personal and not influenced by others.

[17] Some companies report findings to ALL staff.

[18] Collective as used in this book refers to goals or activities that have been agreed on by the group.

[19] Levitt. Ted. 1960. Marketing myopia. Harvard Business Review. 8(July/Aug): 24-47.

[20] Porter, Michael. 1998. Competitive Strategy: Techniques For Analyzing Industries and Competitors. New York: Free Press. 396 p.

[21] Suggest reading: Blanchard, K.; O'Connor, M. 1997. Managing by values. San Francisco; Berrett-Koechler. 157 p.

[22] Arrien, Angeles. 1993. The Four-Fold Way: Walking the paths of the Warrior, Teacher, Healer, and Visionary. San Francisco: HarperCollins. 224 p.

[23] Redfield, James. 1993. The Celestine Prophecy: An Adventure. New York: Warner Books. 256 p.

[24] Reminder, Conditions Of Satisfaction = COS

[25] On price delivery assumes that the process is productive – but additional wording can be valuable or necessary depending on exact nature of the organization.

[26] Suggested reading: Kotler, Philip; Keller, Kevin 2012. Marketing Management (14th Edition). Upper Saddle River, NJ: Prentice Hall, Inc. 816 p.

[27] Fulgham, Robert. 2004. All I Really Need to Know I Learned in Kindergarten. New York: Ballantine Books.

[28] Ivan Pavlov, 1927 Classical Conditioning or Stimulus-Response Theory of Behavior.

[29] Sir Isaac Newton formulated the Black Box Theory of Science suggesting that natural phenomena follow a sequence of "input to black box to output" to explain how things happen, but not why things happen in science.

[30] A test drive is a physical attention getting stimulus rather than the "trial" step in the adoption process. The trial stage would be when a car is purchased for the first time.

[31] Scott "Carrot Top" Thompson is a nationally renowned red headed comedian.

[32] Pride, W.M.; Ferrell, O.C. 1991. Marketing concepts and strategies. Boston: Houghton Mifflin. 739 p.

[33] Land, George; Jarmin, Beth. 1992. Breakpoint and beyond: mastering the future – today. New York: Harper Business. 261 p.

[34] Reminder that products in this context refer to "bundles of benefits" and thus apply to services as well.

[35] Womack, James P.; Jones, Daniel T. 2003. Lean Thinking: Banish waste and create wealth in your corporation, 2nd Edition. New York: Free Press. 379 p.

[36] This example does not apply to the "super custom" manufacturers that rarely use the same material twice nor produce the same or even similar product twice.

[37] LEAN Enterprise Institute

[38] Covey, Stephen M.R. 2006. The Speed of Trust: The one thing that changes everything. New York: Free Press. 354 p.

[39] Thomas, Kenneth W. 2002. Introduction To CONFLICT Management: Improving performance using the TKI. Mountain View, CA: CPP, Inc. 44 p.

[40] Also see: Patterson, Kerry; Grenny, Joseph; McMillan, Ron; Switzler, Al. 2012. Crucial Conversations: Tools for Talking When the Stakes Are High. New York: McGraw-Hill. 233 p.

[41] Patterson, Kerry; Grenny, Joseph; McMillan, Ron; Switzler, Al. 2004. Crucial Confrontations: Tools For Resolving Broken Promises, Violated Expectations and Bad Behavior. New York: McGraw-Hill. 256 p.

[42] This saying has been attributed to Albert Einstein, Mark Twain, Benjamin Franklin and the "Chinese." There appears little agreement on where it actually originated.

CPSIA information can be obtained
at www.ICGtesting.com
Printed in the USA
LVHW01s2220170118
563078LV00003B/211/P